GETTING OUT OF BUFFALO

A MEMOIR OF
FAMILY SECRETS

LEE MARSH

iUniverse, Inc.
New York   Bloomington

Getting out of Buffalo
A MEMOIR OF FAMILY SECRETS

iUniverse books may be ordered through booksellers or by contacting:

iUniverse
1663 Liberty Drive
Bloomington, IN 47403
www.iuniverse.com
1-800-Authors (1-800-288-4677)

Because of the dynamic nature of the Internet, any Web addresses or links contained in this book may have changed since publication and may no longer be valid. The views expressed in this work are solely those of the author and do not necessarily reflect the views of the publisher, and the publisher hereby disclaims any responsibility for them.

ISBN: 978-1-4502-5501-1 (sc)
ISBN: 978-1-4502-5502-8 (ebook)

Printed in the United States of America

iUniverse rev. date: 09/14/2010

Some names and places have been changed
for reasons of privacy

With love, (and thanks to my wife, Renie, especially for her editorial suggestions) and to my children, Suzanne and Jon.

If your ship doesn't come in,
swim out to it.

Jonathan Winters
....

Be glad you're neurotic.

Louis Bisch, M.D.
....

Prologue

In 1948, when I was thirteen, my Schwinn bike took me everywhere.

Delaware park was only fifteen minutes away. I skated there on the ice, spending more time on the insides of my ankles than on the blades, never failing to notice, however, the calves of the young girls flitting around on the ice like nymphs in a Greek opera. They giggled at the intentional stares of a skinny kid just getting seriously interested in the opposite sex.

At the Buffalo Zoo, danger lurked on the other side of the iron bars and glass enclosures. But Eddie the Chimp was my friend. We were the same age. He ate bananas, smiled with crooked yellow teeth and looked at me pleadingly with watery brown eyes. I could have sworn he was trying to say: "Get me out of here!"

Exactly the way I felt about Buffalo.

I lived on an average street in an average house, had a loving mother who listened to my problems, a father who tolerated me, except when he didn't, and a pretty sister who liked me, except when I invaded her turf. The winters were cold but the house was warm enough and every pleasant summer we all went to Niagara Falls, ate at Louis Restaurant, and then watched millions of gallons of water plunge to the river below.

Despite the good times, there was, however, another place in which I spent my young life, a parallel universe, the city of a teenager uneasily coming of age, buffeted by family discord and often by a few bad animals of the human kind.

My mother sympathized with my growing pains. "Someday you'll write stories about everything you're experiencing now, and you'll laugh."

She said this more than once and I believed her because she had never lied to me. I had, in fact, written a few minor things and imagined myself someday as an author of books. And so, each night for months, I went to bed vowing to begin writing on a regular basis. My first story, whenever I would start it, would be a true one about a boy named Calvin who kept saying that I had "killed Christ." On the advice of my father, a lawyer, I had always denied it, usually while running at full speed.

My father took a few minutes one day between trials to help me out, explaining that Jesus had died almost two thousand years ago so that, logically, it was physically impossible that I had had anything to do with his death. My mother pulled me aside and said that the Romans had done it. One day, Miss Lemke, my grammar school teacher, said that Jesus was still living. It was all very confusing to someone like myself who could barely get out of grammar school and never really understood that much about organized religion anyway.

At night, upset by my thoughts, I played mind games in bed that had me escaping from Buffalo for distant shores I might never see except in the movies of Dorothy Lamour and Jon Hall. I usually landed on an undiscovered island in the Pacific, alone, eating the fruit of coconuts fallen recently from palm trees, so different from the old elm in front of my house. Sometimes, on my island, I played the part of Robinson Crusoe, surviving everything nature could throw at me. Occasionally I saw Tarzan swimming by in the surf out beyond the coral reefs while Superman flew overhead to see what all the fuss was about.

Weaving in and out of these fantasies were seemingly unanswerable questions: Why was I the daily object of another boy's hate? And why did I feel so out of place in the city of my birth? Could the answers lie somewhere in my past?

Chapter one

Christmas vs. Hanukkah

I don't know exactly when I first became aware of Christmas… or that I was missing out on something. It was probably a cold Buffalo weekend in December, sitting next to my father in the front seat of his brand new 1939 Pontiac. It was a rare occasion and I was happy to be alone with him, just the two of us. We were on our way downtown to the Ellicott Square Building where he shared an office with another lawyer. Along the way, on Main Street, wild eyed men in long white beards and red suits waived at us and I was curious.

"Look Daddy. That man has a red suit on."
"That's Santa."
"There's another red man."
"Santa," My father repeated impatiently.
"He's Santa too?"
"Uh huh."
"Why?"
"Umm… I don't know. Ask your mother."

"What does Santa do, Daddy?"

"He gives presents at Christmas."

"Do I get presents for Christmas?"

"Um…No."

"Why not , Daddy?"

"Jewish people don't get presents at Christmas."

"Why not?"

"Well…umm… we have Hanukkah."

"I get presents for Han… kah?"

"I don't know. Ask Mommy."

"Look Daddy. There's another Santa."

"Uh huh."

On Saturdays, afraid that the Depression might return, my father often went down to his office to work and to review his visible assets. I remember only two or three times when he took me along with him. I suppose his intention was to show my mother that he had at least some instincts of fatherhood. Most of the time I felt like I was a major annoyance to my father, a veteran of the Great Depression, who was seriously concerned about making a living for a family of four. At the office, he would bring out his files from a green metal cabinet. Each represented a potential future source of income. I would sit there quietly, watching him, inhaling the stale air of the room, listening as he uttered words I didn't quite understand. Still… he was talking to me.

"This is a pretty good case," he'd say, eyeing me tentatively. Was he asking me or telling me? Did he want my opinion?

"Don't accept any less than five thousand," I might have said twenty years later when I had some knowledge of the law and proclivities of juries. But I just nodded and said nothing.

Even at five, when my father sounded stressed, I knew enough not to talk.

For an hour or so, he'd review each file, make a few rhetorical comments, and write down some thoughts and numbers on the inside flap of the file. Then he'd replace the files in the cabinet. In his car again, he'd drive around for a while and stop at a tire store or doctor's office, introduce himself, then hand out business cards with his name on it. He was very friendly to people he had just met, I thought. Sometimes, even on holidays when the courts were closed and other men were out building snow men with their children or taking them on picnics at Ellicott Creek, he would work. He reminded me, shortly before his death, how he had once taken me to a black funeral home on William Street. He was warmly welcomed by an elderly colored gentleman who happened to be the owner. A few months before, the man had referred a woman to him. The woman's husband had been hit by a bus and killed. Now, on Christmas day, my father handed the owner a gift wrapped in colorful holiday paper, together with a sealed envelope which he opened. The man smiled broadly with large white teeth covering most of his dark face. Then he took my father's hand and mine and the three of us walked over to a mourning black couple sitting in the front seats near an open casket.

"This is Mr. Marsh," he said to the bereaved couple. "He's the best lawyer in town . He handles accident cases just like the one that killed your son. He may be able to help you."

Maybe it was that day I suspected in my unformed child's mind that Santa wasn't always the color of red.

My father was a Mason. He joined the Masonic Order toward the last days of the Depression, hoping to raise his annual income. He didn't realize he would also enjoy the meetings. The Masons allowed only Protestants and Jews to belong. Catholics had the

Knights of Columbus to themselves. Discriminated most of his life, he had joined an exclusionary club. No Catholics allowed. He was welcomed at the Masons, the only Jew in the club, the only lawyer. Members asked him legal questions, no fee attached. It was a little flattering to be the legal mind of last resort for the local chapter.

The Masons had a secret handshake that my father was reluctant to disclose, even when I was older. I pestered him for years to let me in on it. But he had given his word to the Order. One day over a cup of coffee, when he was old and quite sick and we had reconciled, he made reference to the Masons, then took my hand in a slightly peculiar way and winked. His tired gray eyes looked at me squarely. "It's good to have a son," he said.

As I grew older, the expression "Merry Christmas" always evoked thoughts of a movie family sitting around a fireplace, warmed not so much by the roaring fire as by the feeling of closeness and love that seemed to pervade the atmosphere. Bing Crosby was there in the background, singing "White Christmas" while Scrooge was ensconced next to Tiny Tim at Bob Cratchett's home with a large dead goose or two in his arms. It was impossible, even as a Jew, not to feel warm and fuzzy at this time of year.

I always wondered, though, why there was nothing in the movies or on radio programs about Hanukkah, the stunning ancient victory of the Jewish Maccabees over the Syrians. The holiday my mother had told me about was as invisible as Matzo ball soup at the Vatican.

Miss Lemke, my teacher, never mentioned Hanukkah. She didn't like Jews, Hacky, my best friend, thought because of the way she pronounced his last name. "Henry Goldsteeeen," she'd say, dragging out his last name with her high screechy voice.

"Read the next line to the class, Henry..ee."

7

Actually, I think she had a defect in her jaw that prevented her from closing her mouth properly. A religious bigot…or not, I was sure that she didn't like me any more than Hacky. After all, I had nearly driven her crazy with my incessant talking in class. When I turned silent it was only because I was concentrating on Sally Pearl's lovely legs on the other side of the room crossing and uncrossing with machine like precision. This, instead of paying attention to the wisdom erupting from my teacher's mouth.

Two weeks before Christmas : I was thinking about the approaching vacation and Sally, and not much else until I heard my name called .

"Leeeee, did you hear what I said?"

I raised my head, surprised. "Umm…Yes, Miss Lemke."

"What did I sayeeeee?"

"Umm…"

"You didn't hear me, did you ?"

She had me. "I guess not, Miss Lemke."

"Why not?"

"I think I might have, umm…wax in my ears."

This evoked several snickers from my classmates.

"And nothing in between them, apparently. How are you ever going to get out of grammar school and go on to high school if you never listen to what I say?"

Cold sweat dripped down my legs. Or was it something else?

"Next time I'll try to listen to what you say."

"It's too late for that. I think it's a good time to stand out side in the hall. Your favorite spot. You can listen to the class singing Christmas songs from there. A minute later, I was crouching alone in a dark corner of the hall, listening with one ear to the beautiful sounds of "Silent Night," "Hark the Herald Angels Sing," and

"Little town of Bethlehem." My other ear was reserved for Mrs. Plasky making her rounds. The sounds of swishing emanating from the principal's voluminous thighs brushing against each other as she approached had always put fear in my heart. Sitting in the hall, I questioned why this had happened to me. I just wanted to be liked by my teachers. By everyone. I suspected that Jesus, about whom the class was singing, had once also had the same feelings of alienation. Could the two of us possibly be related in some way, separated only by a couple thousand years of suffering? Were we so different, he and I ?

1. He was Jewish, just like me.

2. He was a carpenter and built things. I also had some experience in that very area with my Lincoln Log set.

3. He had enemies and so did I .

4. He never married and I suspected my prospects were negligible.

5. He walked on water while I skated quite well on frozen water.

6. He loved the poor. My father, whenever I asked him for money, always swore we were one of them.

7. Finally... according to Miss Lemke, Jesus had always turned the other cheek. Hadn't I tried to do the very same thing whenever Calvin dragged me to the ground and slapped my face ?

Sitting in the corner, waiting for Mrs. Plasky to appear, I realized I might have been happy growing up as a Christian. Calvin wouldn't have given me nightmares and Jesus would have been my "buddy" instead of a hurdle to cross. And I would have had that glorious holiday, Christmas, just like my Gentile classmates. Thinking about it now, no matter how many times Calvin and his friends chased me home from school, no matter how many times Miss Lemke threw me out of her class, I never thought badly of Christians, or of Jesus. I just wondered, sometimes, about the disconnect between Him and a few of his twentieth century followers.

When I was ten, I wanted a Christmas tree. All the other boys in the neighborhood had one. Why not me? I asked my mother. She thought for only a moment, then agreed.

My father heard about this and protested. "We're Jewish," he said. They argued back and forth, like always.

"You haven't been to temple in years" my mother reminded him, to which he had no answer.

It seems my father was just as uncomfortable about me getting a Christmas tree as he had been with his religion after his Bar Mitzvah in 1913. During Yom Kipper, he was shocked to see the Cantor eating in the back room of the Synagogue just before he was scheduled to sing the Kol Nidre.

"Benny… " the Cantor pleaded…"You don't understand. If I don't eat, I can't sing."

Apparently, my father didn't understand that kind of logic and never forgave him, nor apparently the religion, which he said, until his death, was a "business like General motors." My mother always said that he just didn't want to pay the Temple dues.

Over his objections, though, when I was ten, I got my tree.

The small spruce was placed in the window of our living room. It was no taller than I was but I didn't care. Ten days before December 25th, my mother and I decorated the tree with all the excitement of our Christian neighbors. Just like their trees, the Silver tinsel and red and green lights hung from each branch. At the top we attached a star. Underneath the tree there were presents. When my father got home, he looked at the tree, shrugged his shoulders and said simply, "Nice Hanukkah bush."

Chapter two

Running in place

I was moving fast, not fast enough. He was gaining on me. This wasn't one of those Saturday afternoon adventure movies I watched with my friend Hacky in cloistered safety at the Shea's Buffalo. Calvin was very real. And dangerous. "You dirty Jew," he screamed wildly, close now.

Since he had moved to Buffalo three years before, my seventh grade classmate had taught me about the nature of prejudice. "You killed Christ, the Jews killed Christ," he growled in an ugly mantra of hate. I reflexively turned to see his clenched teeth and mouth locked in a satanic grin. From past experience, I knew what was coming next.

"Get away from me. You're crazy, I didn't kill anybody," I hollered as he tackled me in the snow. I swung at his distorted face. My right hand brushed his left eye. He winced enough to give me some satisfaction. But it was no use. He was too big. He pinned my arms under his knees and slapped my face until I bled. I thought of screaming for help but my father's admonition, "Be a man," flashed across my brain like words on a cue card.

At home, my mother saw the congealed blood and knew what had happened. "Oh God," she groaned. "I'm going to say something to his mother." She pulled me toward her. "I know you've told me not to say anything but he keeps hurting you Lee. Look at your lip and your eye."

"It's okay, mom," I said, "It's really okay."

That evening, from my secret hiding place at the top of the stairs, I nursed my wounds quietly and watched my parents in the living room below failing to connect with each other, as usual.

"You know," my mother said, disgusted, in a venue where she couldn't win, "Why do so many people in this country think the Jews are responsible for everything…wars, the bad economy, their jobs, even something that happened two thousand years ago?"

My father had heard this story from my mother before. He pulled his head out of a legal brief, obviously annoyed. "Fanny, wake up, there's nothing we can do about what they think. So forget about it. I forgot about it a long time ago."

It was obvious that the subject had become annoying and mostly irrelevant to his life.

My mother looked away, suddenly quiet. Had he won the argument? My father always did what he wanted to do anyway, and she had usually gone along with him, starting in 1939 when he bought the house on Summer Road. She hadn't wanted to live there, several miles from her friends and the temple. But the price at $4,900 had been too good to pass up, at least from my father's point of view. Nine years later, we lived in the same place.

"You're defending them," my mother said, regrouping .

"I'm defending the right to get some work done so I can support us and send Lee to College someday." He shook his head. He had a big trial coming up.

But my mother refused to let it go. "At least, you have to admit, we have to do something about that Calvin boy."

"We don't have to do anything," my father said, lashing out at her. You're always protecting your son but he's thirteen now.

Whatever he's going through will toughen him up for the real world out there, the world I live in. You forget that some of my clients call me the 'Jew lawyer' behind my back. I'm used to it. Probably a quarter or half of Buffalo is anti-Semitic anyway. Why should some of the kids in this neighborhood be any different than my clients?"

"Your clients don't physically assault you, as far as I know."

"I've had a few close calls."

"Okay, Ben, forget it," she said angrily. "Lee will be okay. He just has to learn to run a little faster."

My father hunched his shoulders, threw off the sarcasm and guilt and returned to his brief.

"What about Lee's Bar Mitzvah?"

"Christ," he groaned, "can't you leave me alone? "

Maybe he had forgotten that the world was expecting me to become a "man" soon. But my mother had uttered the dreaded words that represented dollars flying out of his wallet faster than the cases coming in.

"We can't afford it right now. We'll talk about it again."

"When?" she persisted.

"When I get ready to," he said uncomfortably.

"I hope I'll still be alive at the time," my mother said.

"If you don't stop talking, I'll be beating you to the grave," my father said disgusted. He picked up his trial material and retreated toward the bedroom, cursing under his breath, partly in the Yiddish he had learned from his parents.

My mother worried about me, just as she would eighteen

years later in the intensive care ward of Buffalo General Hospital, wondering how her son would ever be able to carry on without her. I was a lawyer then, trained in logic, but for weeks still unable to cope with the mystery of death.

Chapter three

Family Secrets

I said before that my best friend was Hacky Goldstein but I had another friend, Danny who was thirteen and studying for his Bar Mitzvah, an event which would take place at Temple Emanuel in three months. Danny's father, Jack Gelman, owned a very successful bakery store and had "money," as my father would say when talking about anyone he perceived to have deeper pockets than his own. Along those lines, my uncle Sy, who looked up to nothing but a good horse and often gambled and lost at the track in Batavia sometimes remarked with his unique brand of humor that he (also) had "money ...but not very much." Anyway, Mr. Gelman lived well, enjoyed life and was a prominent member, with his wife, of the Temple of which my family could only be occasional visitors since my father had never wanted to pay the Temple dues.

In spite of our "exclusion" from Temple activities, my mother's talent in playing the Piano and her recognition as President of the local chapter of the Denver Home had enabled her to break into the upper crust of Jewish society in Buffalo. In addition, she had done a great deal of work over the years accompanying prominent singers on the piano, one of which was the Cantor who had an attractive baritone voice and sometimes sang for groups outside of the Temple.

One day, concerned about my future, my mother swallowed her pride and asked the Cantor if he could suggest something as to how I might have a Bar Mitzvah at the Temple in view of the fact that our family didn't belong, and, as she put it, "my husband has no intention of joining."

The good Cantor stroked his chin, taking a minute to evaluate her predicament, then asked "Do you know Evelyn Gelman?"

"Very well," my mother said."She's a member of my club, I'm the President. Why do you ask?"

"Well, I don't think Mrs. Gelman would mind if your son shared the spotlight for ten minutes at Daniel's Bar Mitzvah which is coming up. I'd be glad to teach your son enough Hebrew to get by."

"That's wonderful , but I'm a little concerned about doing this. Are you pretty sure she or her son won't mind?"

"I think so. I'll put in a good word for you. If everything is okay I'll let you know and you can then call Mrs. Gelman to discuss the arrangements."

The following week, Evelyn Gelman graciously agreed to allow me to infringe on her son's special day. I wasn't sure how Danny felt about it, though, and I was too embarrassed to ask.

Finally, the big day arrived. Because of the unusual circumstances, I had told almost no one of the drama unfolding, mostly in my own mind. Family and friends that might have otherwise been invited knew nothing of the event. Dressed in my freshly ironed dark suit, I sat uneasily next to my parents and sister, seven rows behind the Gelmans, while their son on the bima nervously chanted the music and words he had been taught.

Then it was my turn. The Rabbi coughed a little. Maybe he was as nervous as I. Maybe he wondered, as I did, what I was doing there.

"Lee Marsh, Daniel's friend," he said, "will now join in this day of celebration of his manhood."

I walked to the bima, looking back at my family for support. They smiled proudly. I still felt wildly uncomfortable, certain I was diminishing the real Bar Mitzvah boy's moment. Certainly that would be the case when I opened my mouth to sing since his singing voice was no match for mine. Desperate to conclude the event as quickly as possible with as little effect on our disintegrating friendship, I rushed through the chants, sometimes intentionally going off key. No one seemed to notice. My mother's eyes glowed approval. Unfortunately, everything was going disturbingly right. I finished and the Rabbi smiled, and shook my hand. I turned and walked to my seat as fast as I could, trying hard not to look at my friend.

Forty years later, I was surprised to see his name in a national magazine. I had almost forgotten about the long ago "incident" and was happy to see he had risen to great prominence in the business world. As I read the article, I suddenly realized I still retained some negative feelings about what had transpired when we were both young. I decided to call him at his company in California so that I could say hello and then blubber some kind of long overdue apology. Possibly I could get this monkey off my back once and for all. His secretary put me through to him and he answered as if he had been waiting for my call.

"Is this Dan Gelman ?" I asked tentatively.

"Uh…Yes, this is he."

"Dan. This is Lee Marsh," I said warmly.

"Who?"

"Lee Marsh. From Buffalo. I saw a business article about you recently and wanted to say hello."

"I see...What can I do for you?"

"You remember me, don't you ?" I said, mystified.

"Well.... Not really."

"We had our Bar Mitzvah together in Buffalo. Lee. Lee Marsh."

"Oh," he said flatly. "Lee. The Bar Mitzvah. Yes. Yes. That was a long time ago... A long time ago. Well, it was awfully nice hearing from you, and I'm sorry I can't talk but I have an appointment and have to go now."

The hard click in my ear only bothered me for an hour or so...

No one in my mother's family ever seemed to remember his or her age. Maybe it was because they didn't want to grow old and just didn't want to remember that they had once decided to forget. In any event, they chose not to break the unwritten family rule: SPEAK NOT OF BIRTH DATES. I never really understood this until recently, now that I'm receiving Social Security checks every month and feel the encroachment of arthritis in various parts of my arms, legs, neck and back.

I vaguely remember my grandfather on my mother's side. Samuel was a short man, 5'6" , but apparently a big man in bed. Not that I ever talked with him about that subject, but eleven children springing from his loins speaks for itself, eleven children who weren't sure how old they were.

In the 1940's and 1950's, all of the sons and daughters of Sam and Lina were still alive. Periodically, most of the family gathered in Rochester, New York to bond anew and to wonder, since the last time, what kept them all so young and vibrant at their undisclosed ages. Usually, most of my cousins and I were invited to be part of this great celebration of life and partial amnesia.

These Rochester meetings were something special, where twenty or thirty of us crowded into the home of my Uncle Benny, or Aunt Edith, or sometimes, my cousin Dolly's, Libby's daughter. It must have been disturbing to some of my Aunts, whom I hadn't seen for months, to be asked personal questions by their curious nephew (me) :

"Aunt Paula? "

"What is it dear?"

"Could I ask you a question?"

"Of course, dear."

"How old are you?"

"I don't know dear."

"Why not?"

"I Don't know why I don't know."

"Why not?"

"I don't know, dear. By the way, why aren't you playing with your cousins?"

"I don't know, either. "

We came from everywhere to be together again in Rochester, reversing for a few days the Diaspora that had transported some of us to more glamorous areas of the country. More than a few family members had been seduced in the forties and fifties by the excitement of Southern California.

Paula, a widow whose husband, Alfred, had once received a Warner Brothers acting contract in Hollywood, was there for a time until she remarried and moved to Michigan. Margo, a beautiful woman and the youngest of my aunts, had gone to

Hollywood for a while to enjoy the glamour and once even dated Bruce Cabot, a famous movie star. Occasionally, I see him on late night TV in some old movie like the original "King Kong", and think of my aunt by his side at the Coconut Grove or wherever movie people went in those days. More permanent residents of California were my aunt Mary and her husband, Burt, (a "Ripley's believe it or not" recipient for consecutive football field goals at Rutgers University in the thirties.) Also there was my aunt Bessie who apparently liked California, and her daughter, my cousin Geri, who chose to leave the small town of Lockport (near Buffalo) for Los Angeles in the late 40's, and had made her own wonderful life in the sun, never looking back.

Meanwhile, my uncle Al, a pharmacist and the only "professional" on my mother's side of the family remained in Elmira, while Harry stayed in Ithaca. Uncle Sy, who had in 1903 saved his baby sister (my mother) from certain death by drowning on the boat from Europe, remained in Batavia, refusing to abandon the race track and the horses he loved. Finally, there was my aunt Libby, who often vacationed in the summer in Miami Beach with her mink hanging from her shoulders, and my uncle Benny and aunt Edith, both of whom seemed to always be in Rochester, only sixty miles away, welcoming us whenever we showed up.

Sometimes, late at night and unable to sleep, I think of them all, especially the women, beautiful and ageless, the way they always wanted to be. Then I reel off in my mind the names of my cousins, the sons and daughters of the sons and daughters of Sam and Lina and I go to sleep, satisfied that I am part of the history that started with my grandparents in Russia.

Not long ago, Geri sent me a Naturalization certificate signed by our mutual grandparents in 1916 when Thomas Woodrow Wilson was still President. The ages of the eleven children jumped out at me like a Jack in the Box. Recorded on the old form was my mother's age, "13," making her, as she lay dying in a Buffalo hospital, officially 62 years of age. It was a fact she whispered to me very quietly so no one would hear...

My aunt Libby's husband owned a cigar store in Rochester. He was an amiable man who never had a problem with me handling the cash register every time I arrived, starting when I was about eleven. Selling the cigars to customers of the store and then hearing the loud clanging sound of the register as I pressed the right keys, was always exciting to me.

I couldn't believe it but my uncle usually left the store soon after I got there, trusting me to manage the establishment for several hours. I took the responsibility seriously and was very careful to count out the few coins that came in and put them in their proper places in the cash drawer. I never had a problem. Maybe that was because most of the customers coming into the store only looked at the cigars in the showcase as they walked by me, then went out through the back door of the store without buying anything. As a result, usually I was taking in only three or four dollars on a good day and curious as to how my aunt and uncle were maintaining their existing lifestyle. I was doing almost as well in Buffalo with boys my age, pitching pennies against a wall .

One Saturday afternoon we went to Rochester for a wedding. My father and mother were supposed to meet some friends before the reception, and they dropped me off at the cigar store. My uncle was there and, as usual, soon left through the back way. It was a slow day and I was bored until I heard loud noises coming through the door. Upon opening it, I was surprised to see, not the outside of the store as I expected, but a large room with my uncle and a small group of men inside, several of whom were writing strange words in white chalk on several blackboards.

My uncle caught me gawking, rushed over and quickly led me back into the cigar store proper. "That's just some people having fun, playing a game, just like you play monopoly," he said. I nodded as if I suddenly understood everything, but understood nothing. Later, I asked my father about what I had seen. He said I shouldn't say anything to anyone because "that is how your uncle makes a living, betting on horse racing, and besides, it isn't any of our business anyway."

I had discovered something I wasn't supposed to know or ever talk about, and mostly I never have. I can keep a secret. I'm pretty sure everyone's gone on to that big track in the sky where no one ever loses, and I suppose, for that reason, no one will mind if I say something now, not even the horses.

Chapter four
Looking for heroes

When I was young, I had a great respect for Native Americans.
The cowboy and Indian movies I often saw at the Shea's Buffalo
theater first made me appreciate these unlikely heroes. The way
I saw it, they were a trustworthy bunch who respected the terms
of a treaty, took care of their own and wanted only to be left
alone with their traditions while white men in these movies were
sometimes portrayed as immoral, raping women and stealing
land, occasionally with the help of the U.S. army. The Indian
chiefs I admired so much are now melded in my mind into a
single composite figure . He is an old man with a weathered face,
bloodshot eyes that had seen every inequity to his people, and
a knack for listening patiently to the younger, more excitable
members of the tribe who often wanted only revenge for the
injustices inflicted on them by the white man. I remember this
man mumbling words of restraint, something like my grandfather
on my father's side, who, in the midst of family arguments, would
say "sha." (Be quiet, calm down, take it easy, life's too short.)
Summer Road where I lived might have been part of an old

Indian name from the city's past, rooted in the history of the Seneca nation which had inhabited the area in the century before I was born. Elk and deer, I liked to think, must have run free on the same dirt on which I now fled almost daily from Calvin.

Not far from my house was Miller's Pharmacy. Each week, doing everything I could to avoid detection, I evaluated the most recent lot of ten cent comic books that old Mr. Miller had chosen to stack on the revolving stand. Occasionally, when quarters or halves fell unnoticed from my father's pants the night before, I might even buy a "Captain Marvel" or (more likely) a "Superman," my favorite of all the super heroes. After all, the "Man of Steel" had talents Captain Marvel could only dream about. Not only could he climb tall buildings with a single bound but he could stop a speeding locomotive with his bare hands. Bullets had no affect on his powerful body. His accomplishments were even greater. Once, in a 1940's Look Magazine article, I read that he (and I) had flown across the Atlantic Ocean to Germany to capture Adolph Hitler. After that, my imagination knew no bounds.

One day, feeling like my indestructible hero, I climbed to the top of my parent's dresser with a pillow case. Holding it high above my head I jumped, expecting trapped air to allow me to float gracefully to the floor below. Unfortunately, the pillow case refused to open. Plummeting into the sharp wooden point of the bedpost below, my right eye disappeared behind a pool of blood just as my mother arrived in the room and joined me in screaming at the tops of our voices. Eight stitches later, I left the hospital with my eye in tact, still available for the purpose it was intended by God or possibly by the rulers of Krypton.

Every fall I played touch football on the street in front of my house. Out of embarrassment, Calvin never played with our small group or even showed his face because he and Jack Hupp, our star receiver, had once had a disagreement in which Jack had permanently moved Calvin's nose a half inch closer to his left ear. To play Street Football was to try and catch a "pigskin" running at full speed while avoiding oncoming cars. It was a sport right up there with sky diving and kissing King Cobras. Several close calls occurred, one in which part of my jacket attached itself to a bumper. Luckily, it tore loose almost immediately or I'd have set a new world record for the fifty yard dash.

Our quarterback, Phil Valloni, knew I had a talent for running fast but wasn't very good at catching footballs. He was fair about it though, thinking that I might get lucky and catch one once in a while. Usually, he threw to Hupp, who was big for his age and must have had Elmer's glue on his fingers. He caught everything Phil threw his way. Jack could have played for the first team at Notre Dame and someone said he actually did. There were others in our group like Bob Thomas and Leo Murphy whose faces and resumes have blurred over the years but they were all pretty good athletes and got plenty of balls thrown their way. In a way, they were all my heroes because I admired them for their athleticism.

We never discussed anything about religion but I think they knew I was Jewish because every few weeks we'd swim naked (as was the custom) at the YMCA. Their uncircumcised appendages flopped around conspicuously, while mine stuck out like a sore thumb.

My friend, Henry (Hacky) Goldstein, lived four blocks from me on Woodland Lane where the houses were beautiful and no one played in the streets, not even the dogs. The homes there were a lot more expensive than those on Summer Road, mostly red brick, with manicured, green lawns in the summer. In contrast, our lawn was the color of hay because I never watered it .

I looked up to Hacky in more ways than one. For starters,

he was six inches taller than me. (Despite my having received a few growth hormone injections from our family doctor with the encouragement of my worried mother, I would remain undersized for my age until I arrived in high school.) Hacky lived up to his elevated stature, walking with a slow, deliberate gait, which I admired and sometimes tried to imitate. Looking like John Wayne in "Red River," his size and manner discouraged anyone from challenging him to a fight or bothering me when I was with him. Without knowing it, he had become my unofficial bodyguard.

He and I often imagined what we'd do when we "grew up." Hacky's father owned a jewelry store on Main Street. He wanted him in the business someday. But Hacky had told his father he wouldn't do it.

"You're crazy," I said one day. "I'd love to work there."

"If you knew my father, you wouldn't say that. Anyway, I'm going to be a pilot, and fly people around the country, like my uncle."

"Jewish guys don't became pilots," I said. But my words were jealous ones because Hacky at least knew what he wanted to be. I had no idea. I figured I wasn't getting out of the eighth grade alive anyway, if Cal had his way.

But on the bus one day, I saw a pretty girl across the aisle intently reading a book and ignoring my stares.

"Maybe I'll be a writer, like Ernest Hemingway," I said a little louder than necessary, hoping she'd look up.

"Who?" Hacky said.

It was obvious he had never heard of Hemingway while I had had the advantage of my mother's broad interest in literature. A few of the famous author's novels rested with others on our bookshelf at home. Recently, at my mother's suggestion, I had looked at his fictional story about a Jew named Cohn, and his friend Jake. It had intrigued me because Cohn had proved himself adept as a boxer, redeeming himself with his bullying gentile classmates at Princeton. I got through about eight pages before returning to my comics, but I would remember Cohn, and "The Sun Also Rises." Maybe, somewhere, there was hope for me.

Chapter five

Hiding out

Avoiding Calvin on the streets of Buffalo was akin to a well endowed naked Jew in Berlin trying to escape detection in front of Gestapo headquarters .

Then I found the Deco Diner.

It had always been there waiting for me and most of the other kids in my neighborhood with nothing except lint in our pockets.

Once I discovered I had a talent for pitching pennies, I started collecting a few dollars every week speculating on how close to a wall I could toss a coin. Encouraged I graduated to nickels and my income rose accordingly, allowing me to walk into the Deco on Main Street one day for a hamburger and a coke. Ed Kelly, the short order cook, was there, standing behind the counter. He was a big man, over six feet tall and, judging by the size of his stomach, must have been eating most of the food coming off the grill.

"How you doing, Buddy," he said when I first walked in. I looked around to see if he was talking to me. Later, I discovered that he called everyone "Buddy." Maybe he didn't remember names, I thought, but after a while I didn't care. I liked talking with him and got to asking him questions about his life. I was always curious about things like that.

He'd been a boxer in Chicago in the heavyweight division during the Depression. Sometimes, he made as much as a "hundred dollars a night." That was a lot of money in those days. He ate "three squares" a day when other men were selling apples on the corner to survive. Toward the end of the Depression, he got hit by a car outside a bar and had a permanent limp after that and no way to make a living in boxing. The Army didn't want him and he headed for New York. The Deco diner in Buffalo where he stopped on the way served up good coffee and the pretty girl behind the counter who waited on him. The coffee was 5c. She was apparently free and came with a gleam in her Irish green eyes. She also recommended him for a job and then married him. He never left Buffalo or the Deco after that.

About a month after I came to the Deco, I told Ed about Calvin and how he was making my life a living Hell. "He better not come in here," he said. "Somebody did that to me too when I was growing up in Chicago. A Polack. You're not a Polack, are you?" he asked tentatively. I shook my head in denial, although I remembered that some of my family on my father's side had been born in Poland. (Was I therefore a "Polack?" Or just a polish Jew? Was there a difference?)

"There's a lot of them in this town just like Chicago," he said. Some of them are okay. Anyway, this kid calls me a rotten Mick, then slams my head into the ground. He thought he had me scared. He was wrong and I hit him with a right hand so hard I broke his nose. That's when I thought of going into boxing. Anyway, he didn't bother me after that. That's what you got to do, Buddy. Or I'll do it for you if he comes in here when you're here."

"Maybe I'll do it myself," I said with a bravado I didn't quite feel, thinking it might have been safer to jump off the bridge into the Niagara River than to go after Calvin's nose.

When I was eleven, I began writing stories at the Deco, little stories, and Ed would read them and laugh. The ideas were never original beginning with my "great" two pager, "Mother Mahoney's Meatballs" about a boy who loves his mother's meatballs, eats too many, falls asleep and wakes up as a … "meatball." He sweats gravy. Girls don't go near him. His friends laugh at him. Dogs threaten him. About to be eaten by a German Shepherd, he wakes up like Dorothy in the Wizard of Oz, grateful to be alive.

Encouraged, I filched other ideas from movies I saw on Saturday afternoons in the darkness of the Hippodrome theater. Dorothy Lamour and Maria Montez frolicked there in sarongs, far from Buffalo, somewhere South of Tahiti, or ran through Arab harems half naked. If memory serves me correctly, this is what I wrote:

"Lelani's tiny feet splashed through the water of the green lagoon. She had nothing on except a grass skirt held together with coconut rope. She stood for a while with the Dolphins who wanted to be near her, like all the boys of the island who were waiting for her skirt to fall off."

"Makes me want to be there in the water with her," Ed said with a smile across his face.

That was enough for me. Compliments. I liked compliments. After all, I wasn't getting many from my father.

Chapter six

Blood sport

If I was running from Calvin's fists on a regular basis, when it came to watching other boys take a beating, I was somehow more accepting of the blood that flowed. Big fights among teenage boys were not that unusual in the 1940's. Faces and fingers changed shape every day. I was secretly envious of boys who could walk into a fight apparently unafraid of getting smashed on the nose by another boy's knuckles. Their fathers must have been proud of them.

I remember one fight above all. It involved Billy Deveaugh, my seventh grade classmate, and Victor Kasner, a high school freshman.

Everyone knew they hated each other but no one knew why. Billy didn't want to talk about it. He didn't talk much anyway. I think he liked being mysterious like Alan Ladd or Humphrey Bogart acted in those days. Calm, cool and collected. When the word leaked out that the two of them would meet behind the school the following Friday to settle their differences, whatever they were, everyone got excited.

Victor was two years older, three inches shorter and thirty pounds heavier than Billy. His arms were the size of an average gorilla's at the Buffalo Zoo. Associating with a bad crowd on the East side of Buffalo, he had been arrested once for stealing hubcaps from a car but the police couldn't prove it and let him go.

I knew him only because he was Jewish and had seen him a few times at Rhonda Cohen's house. Rhonda had these small parties when her parents were out. Ten or twelve girls and boys would show up for the free food and whatever excitement the opposite sex provided. She was the perfect hostess, even at twelve, a regular Pearl Mesta. She also was a nice girl, pretty with dark hair and a cute figure, who got satisfaction from making her friends happy. I liked her but was annoyed one afternoon when Victor showed up. Later, I found out she hadn't invited him. He had just heard about the party and walked in and no one was big enough to throw him out.

On the day of the big fight, at least thirty boys and girls showed up. Billy's girlfriend, Jean, was there and so was Calvin, but I stayed away from him on the other side of the crowd, like he had the black plague. Everyone gathered in the playground area behind the school and formed a large ring. Billy got there first. It was a warm day in late September and he had on a clean white tee shirt hanging loose outside of his pants. Everyone of us was chanting "Billy, Billy," like he had won already. But none of us had ever seen him fight anyone as big as Victor. After ten minutes, Victor hadn't showed up and we wondered if the fight was going to happen. "Victor's a coward," everyone hollered, at least until he showed up and then the crowd shut up fast. The sleeves of his black shirt were rolled up to show his massive arms. He smiled like a cobra ready to strike, his big head sneering at the hostile crowd.

He would get rid of this thirteen year old upstart, fast. Faster than it took to steal a hubcap.

I was suddenly afraid for Billy. But he stood there as cool as a popsicle and smiled at his girlfriend.

Victor pointed his finger at Billy. "I'll push your face in" he said .

"Let's go then," Billy said calmly.

They circled each other. Billy's hands were tight white fists, waiting to strike. Victor was a dirty fighter. Billy had heard the stories. He suddenly barreled toward Billy like a truck, his head parallel to the ground, aiming for his midsection. Billy was ready for him. He danced aside with the grace of Fred Astaire at the same time as his fist rose from the dirt. He caught Victor on the chin, dropping him to one knee. He wiped the blood from his face. He looked at the crowd, straightened his shoulders, then ran again at Billy, trying to redeem himself. His elbow slammed into Billy's head. Billy looked like he was stunned. Victor closed in but Billy must have been faking because his right hand rocketed toward Victor's nose and struck with a sickening crunch. Blood seeped from his nose. His eyes were wild. His mouth hung open. He was breathing hard.

They circled each other again like Roman gladiators, the only thing missing were the Lions.

Victor had something left. He hit Billy above his left eye with his open hand and pushed his knee into Billy's groin. Billy groaned and went down under the dirty onslaught then rolled out of the way as Victor's foot rushed toward him. He pushed himself up, angry, ramming his fist into Victor's gut while his other hand slammed into victor's face. Blood gushed from the bigger man's nose like a broken water fountain.

"Hit him again, Billy. Hit him again," the crowd yelled.

But it was too late. Victor's legs had buckled under him and he slumped to the ground. It was all over. Everyone knew it. Especially Victor.

Billy stood there for a minute, breathing heavily. He looked at his girlfriend. She was crying. He turned to Victor. "Go back to your high school," he said, his voice cracking. "And don't touch her again."

Billy's secret was out.

Chapter seven

Sally

In our last year of grammar school, Sally Pearl and I had become an unlikely "item," a fact which must have grated badly on Calvin. Here I was, an "undersized ant" to be stepped on when he chose, and there she was, blond and beautiful, looking to me like Veronica Lake with every smile of her straight, white, thirteen year old teeth. I watched him in the classroom, drooling over her like the rest of the boys. She was obviously the most desirable girl at school and for reasons I didn't understand, I was the one walking her home and carrying her books, and praying every morning when I woke up that it would continue.

In school I was a non stop talker, constantly whispering important messages or comments to someone across the aisle, often inviting a strong response from my teacher who seemed to always have the acute hearing of Lassie at 500 yards. Alone with Sally, though, my brain seemed to shut down like a clogged water spigot. I rarely spoke, afraid to spoil whatever it was we had together. It didn't seem to matter to her. She talked for both of us. About anything and everything. About books I hadn't read and places I hadn't been. And I loved each intelligent word that fell from her lips. For a girl still in grammar school, she seemed to know a lot. Gradually, I started to see the value in our arrangement. Now, more than sixty years later, I realize I wanted to be near her then as much as possible. I suppose I must have acted like a dog waiting to be fed.

One day, the meal arrived. Sally had invited me for the first time to her house after school. Her mother was out and the two of us played spin the bottle. We kissed more than once after each of our turns. She was obviously enjoying it, from the way she was breathing heavy. "Where did you learn to kiss like that?" she said.

"From Dennis Morgan," I said, remembering that my actual physical experience of placing my lips on another human being had been fairly limited to my mother and sister and occasionally salivating relatives who thought I was "cute enough to eat ."

She squinted in the funny way that attracted me. "Who?"

"Dennis Morgan . The movie star."

"Oh, him. I don't think you can learn anything from just watching someone kiss. There must be another reason. "

I just nodded. Even at thirteen, I knew when it was smart to say nothing.

After that, she invited me over regularly when her mother was out and one day we were sitting on the floor, a few inches apart, with our legs crossed Indian style. I was trying hard not to stare at the white panties protruding from beneath her skirt. My heart rate soared and I blushed at the thought of increasing the level of our intimacy. She noticed and laughed. "You know, you're the best looking boy in our class," she said.

In June, at our grammar school graduation, Sally and I stood beside twenty eight others, nervously giggling as the photographer instructed us to say "cheese." We were then immortalized in a photo that would last far longer than our innocence. Mrs. Plasky, our principal, was careful to stand outside the critical view of the camera, maintaining to the last her iron grip on the class of 1948. The next day, she handed me my graduation certificate. She had told me once in anger that I would never get out of eighth grade. Now she smiled at me, it seemed, for the first time, probably remembering the stories of juvenile delinquency I had inadvertently given her to relate to her grandchildren.

Then school was out, summer had arrived and Sally and I hadn't spoken for a week. Had she forgotten me already? Something, maybe my natural shyness, kept me from calling her.

On a Saturday morning, I found myself with no girlfriend, yet suddenly "rich." The night before, seven one dollar bills had dropped, unnoticed, from my father's pants. Convinced he wouldn't miss the money, I called Hacky thinking we might go to Crystal Beach, the giant amusement park in Canada. It was a place where one could forget everything for a day, even the loss of one's girlfriend. Hacky and I had been there before on numerous occasions. Without automobiles, the only way to get there was to cross choppy Lake Erie on the Canadiana, a 50 year old iron hulled boat. There was a certain obvious risk in doing this since both Hacky and I were never really positive the frequently shuddering boat would make it to the Canadian side of the lake. In my imagination, I pictured myself clinging helplessly to the railing of this latter day Titanic as it sunk to the bottom.

On the Saturday morning of which I speak, Hacky's house maid, who didn't like me (I was sure), answered the phone.

"He's gone on a trip with his parents," she said in her usual frigid voice.

Disappointed, I hung up and pondered the day without Sally or Hacky but quickly decided to go to Crystal Beach. That's where the action was. Grabbing a light jacket and my money, I climbed the bus for the debarkation point at the foot of Main Street. Once aboard the big ship, its horn belching like an overfed gourmond, we moved slowly from the dock to the deeper waters of the lake. I stood at the railing feeling a kinship with Christopher Columbus who must have felt the same way as I as he had sailed away from the Spanish shore. Brave as I thought I was that day, I still never lost sight of the yellow life preserver hanging from the wall, the one I had decided I would grab in the event I sighted any waves crashing dangerously above the deck.

Ten minutes out, with the strong, fresh smell of lake air bracing me, I was surprised to see Sally Pearl suddenly at my side, smiling and pulling at my hand. In the seclusion of her house, she had given me my first real lesson in sexual awareness and now, with sweet music wafting across the deck of the Canadiana, she led me to the center of the deck where the voice of Nat King Cole, coming from a loudspeaker, caressed us both with "Nature Boy."

> *"There was a boy…a very strange enchanted boy…*
> *and though he wandered very far… very far…*
> *over land and sea… a little shy …and sad of I …"*

I knew he was singing about me as I held Sally's waist very tightly, undulating with the rocking of the boat, trying desperately to hide the bulge in my pants.

Eleven years later on a hot Summer day in July of 1959, I saw Sally reading a book at a corner table of a little restaurant in downtown Buffalo where I had gone to cool off. As part of my obligation to Uncle Sam, I had just completed six months of active duty at Fort Dix, New Jersey replete with deep knee bends, pull ups on the iron bar, and plenty of basic army food all of which had filled me out a bit. I must not have looked quite like the same person she had known once before.

"Hello," I said a little nervously, remembering our moment long ago of childhood intimacy. She looked up blankly from the book . It was obvious she didn't recognize me.

"Lee," I said, and then, embarrassed, she remembered and became overly enthusiastic in inviting me to sit down, which I did. A young blond waitress, not nearly as pretty as Sally, came over to our table and I ordered the same thing Sally was drinking, a coke, and for a minute or so, until the drink came, I felt uncomfortable. I could tell Sally was feeling that way also until she broke the ice and asked me what I had been doing.

I told her right up front that I was a lawyer, hoping that would impress her. But she just said "great" without much behind it. So I told her my tried and true Army story (which I had practiced on others a few times since getting back). It was about the rigors of basic training, and how I had almost "died" on the fields of New Jersey as I crawled under a barbed wire fence while tracer bullets flew 36 inches above my head. My slight exaggerations must have worked because Sally laughed at my "near death" experience and edged toward me a little at the table. We both relaxed a little after that and, sitting there, I realized I had missed her. I asked her about herself. She said she had gone to private school, taken off for almost a year to travel, then decided on her parent's advice to go for an arts degree at the University. She had graduated but hadn't done much of anything else after that except living off her parents and dating a dental student at the school. She showed me a picture of a good looking blond guy in his twenties with a pipe.

I was sorry I had asked because she was as pretty as ever, blue eyes and all, and I felt the same attraction I had felt then. Yet I had to admit that something important was missing... and I think she felt the same way since the conversation was pretty sterile after that. I asked her about the book she was holding which was Steinbeck's "The Moon is down." She was reading it for the second time, she said. I nodded knowingly, as if I had read the book a few times myself although I had never read it even once and didn't care to admit it. Later, I made a mental note to read it, and did. War stories about the Nazis had a certain gruesome appeal to me around that time anyway.

There wasn't much left for either of us to say after that except that the weather was nice and Buffalo's downtown was deteriorating pretty badly. Then I said goodbye, kissed her on the cheek, trying hard not to smell the perfume on her neck, and I left and never saw her again.

Chapter eight

A smokescreen

I was with my mother the day she had a check up with Dr. Montrose. She couldn't exactly describe what was bothering her except to say she felt out of sorts. Dr. Montrose examined her and said she was just smoking too much. Eventually, it would destroy her lungs and kill her. He pulled no punches. Even in front of me.

My mother didn't tell him everything.....that her marriage was falling apart. She was too proud to say this in 1947. Besides, she didn't like to think of things she couldn't do anything about. She left the doctor's office, lit up a cigarette, forgot why she had come, and went on with raising her two children, and doing her charitable club work which gave her pleasure.

She was President of the local chapter of the Denver Home, a national organization which, ironically, rehabilitated lung and tubercular patients from around the country. In Colorado that summer, representing the chapter, she had come away with national recognition.

In the fall, she arranged a charity fundraiser for her club in the form of a concert to be held at Kleinhan's Music Hall with the Buffalo Philharmonic Orchestra as the centerpiece. Because of her talent on the piano, my mother had many close friends in the world of classical and popular music, some with the Philharmonic. The orchestra had agreed to donate it's services for the Club's benefit. Then, a famous singer agreed to sing at the affair. Perry Como was in town on a promotional tour. The Buffalo Evening News said he was staying at the Statler Hotel for the weekend. My mother contacted his assistant. It would mean a great deal, she said, to have a star like Como sing a few songs at Kleinhan's on Saturday night, one night hence. The singer had never heard of the Denver Home but graciously agreed to appear anyway.

I was too young to be there when he was introduced to the surprised audience. My mother said he strode to the stage in his black Hollywood tux, a smile on his handsome movie face. With the orchestra behind him, he sang two songs, "Till the end of time," and "Because." The applause was deafening . When he ended, he paused for a moment, and smiled at my sister sitting in the front row. She slumped in her seat until he motioned for her to come up to the stage. She looked around, surprised, stunned, embarrassed. My mother had forgotten to tell her about a brief conversation she had with Como that morning, including : "My daughter is not only beautiful but she plays the piano, and sings."

On this particular evening, legs shakings slightly under her long gown, my sister climbed the stairs to meet Perry Como's outstretched hand. He kissed her on the cheek, then accompanied her to the waiting Steinway. Many times before, at home, she had sat in front of a baby grand exactly like the one in front of her. Both instruments had eighty eight keys. Thirty six were black and fifty two were white. The only thing different this time were the unnerving faces of hundreds of people staring at her. Then something magical happened. A second after her fingers touched the keys, she relaxed and heard herself singing "Can't help lovin' that man of mine," from Showboat. The applause was genuine and deafening and rang in her ears for weeks.

That winter my mother was still smoking as much as ever and I was hiding the Pall Malls every chance I got. But she always found them and lit up despite my efforts.

In a movie theater, it was easier to forget what Dr. Montrose had said. The projection on a silver screen of a soft westerly wind over a sandy palm tree laden beach seemed to blow the cigarette smoke away. That…plus the weekly Serials, a forerunner of Steven Spielberg's "Indiana Jones" movies.

I remember images of the unconscious P 38 aviator plunging to his certain death. The cockpit in that plane was crowded because I and every other screaming kid around me was in there with the pilot, cringing beside his bloodied face, breathing in the acrid smoke, feeling the gut wrenching unfairness of it all. This episode (and those like it) was a "two nail" day that I would painfully regret after the fact. The following Saturday, the pilot of the plane, obviously blessed by cosmic forces we couldn't understand, awoke to save us all. In succeeding weeks, impossible things kept happening as new, different, and more challenging cliffhangers presented themselves. For example, there I was, bound and blindfolded, standing in front of a Nazi firing squad, or thrown from the top of a mountain without a parachute, or locked in a trunk, Houdini like, beneath 30 fathoms of sea water. In each episode, though, death was mysteriously and miraculously avoided.

On the bus heading home, my friend Hacky, the realist, would sometimes say to me , "That guy would've died in real life," and I would agree. But I prayed we were wrong because the fantasy of those Serials always gave me hope that my mother might actually survive that which the tobacco company and her own unhappiness were doing to her lungs.

Chapter nine
Muscles

In 1948, when Israel was desperately fighting for its life, I had become more concerned with my own personal survival. Calvin's frequent after school attacks were leaving me bloodied. Every shadow behind every tree was him stalking me. Didn't he have a life?

When I got home, it was barely different. My father's belt was coming off his pants more frequently. Among other things, he complained I was spending too much time in our bathroom, unfortunately the only one in the house. From the other side of the locked door, he'd begin what was a familiar cross examination, similar to what he had often done as a lawyer to suspected perjurers in the Erie County Court House…("Are you lying now or were you lying then?") It was a Perry Mason question without a good answer and made the eyes of the average man, with something to hide, glaze over in confusion and uncertainty.

At home, it went like this: "What are you doing in there, and why are you doing it?"

"I'll be out soon," I'd stammer.

"What does that mean?" he'd holler impatiently.

"I'm washing my hands," I'd say nervously, rushing over to the faucet to turn it on.

Years of intimidation and danger like this had made my senses especially acute, like a cat in the wild. I could hear him playing nervously with his belt. And that was that, I thought. Always under the gun. If it wasn't Calvin, it was my father.

One day, I awoke after a sleepless night, realizing that the only way I would survive in a world of nervous fathers and dangerous classmates was to get stronger, both mentally and physically.

The answer, I thought, might be found in an advertisement on the back of a magazine I had discovered in a dentist's office. It had assured me that "no bully would ever throw sand" in my face again. I hadn't been to the beach lately but when I saw the name of Charles Atlas strategically placed above the picture of a bronzed muscular giant, I figured I had discovered a sure thing. All I had to do was buy his book and certain equipment, then follow the easy instructions. It had something to do with lifting 100 lb weights or pulling on metal coils for several months by which time my muscles and my confidence would have expanded geometrically. I analyzed everything in detail, looking for flaws. At first I was excited, but after a thorough examination of the facts I concluded that there was another possibility, to wit: my arms, under the strain, might turn into two useless strands of spaghetti. What advice would Atlas have then for the vegetable I would have become? I wouldn't be able to defend myself against anyone. The whole thing was a problem worthy of King Solomon. Eventually, I forgot about Atlas who probably didn't even exist anyway, and I just kept running for my life which was easier.

Chapter ten

A fragile life

Everything had gone as I had planned. I was sick. Laying in snow and slush can do that to a thirteen year old kid who wants to get out of school. With a mildly sore throat and a small temperature, my mother had let me stay home. Feeling slightly guilty, I sat at the kitchen table, across from her, saying nothing, watching a lone slice of lemon float resiliently at the top of her cup of Lipton tea, impervious to gravity. I had serious matters to discuss but suddenly felt strangely detached from my surroundings as if I could fly away like a bird and no one would notice.

It was quiet. My father had left for work and my beautiful sister (no longer in high school) was upstairs, sleeping off a late night date with one of her boy friends. In my imagination, sometimes I envisioned every horny candidate for her favors trying to get into her underwear. And none succeeding. After all, my sister was a virgin and proud to announce that fact on a semi- monthly basis.

It was one of those cold winter days in Buffalo when the chill pushes under the doors of houses and through their walls.

Nothing would change until April or May when the buds would appear on the trees. Until then, the heat from the strategically placed iron radiators would have to do.

"You look unhappy," my mother said, finally breaking the silence.

I shrugged my shoulders, waiting to be coaxed.

"What's wrong ?" she pleaded.

"It's about you and Dad."

"Oh?" She sounded surprised.

"Last night I heard you fighting."

"We do that a lot lately," she said carefully.

"But you were talking about a woman Dad likes."

"Oh, that. It's nothing," she said cautiously, looking away.

But when she looked back, her gray eyes had misted up a bit and I knew there was some truth to the bitter words I had heard.

"Are you going to leave Dad?" I said bluntly.

She looked up in the air for a moment. "You wouldn't want that. Would you?"

"No."

"Then I don't think I could do that. We've been married a long time, you know."

She had told me what I selfishly wanted to hear. But I knew she was sacrificing her happiness for mine and while I wanted her to be happy because I loved her, I knew I would be lost forever if my parents separated. I looked out the kitchen window toward the Elm tree on our front lawn. There was suddenly something personal and very tragic about the snow covered, gnarled old tree, only a few years older than my mother. It had lived for fifty brutal winters outside our house and now, its weathered branches were bent closer to the ground, something like the woman who sat across from me.

This wasn't the first time we had talked over tea and cocoa. She had often helped me cope with my uneven life. But there were times also when I had asked her about herself and I had always felt good about doing that small favor for her because I knew she enjoyed talking about her past :

She was pretty and laughed easily. At 22, Fanny had reasons to be happy. She lived in a nice house on Chase Park in Batavia, New York with her parents, Sholom and Lina Wurtzman, her four brothers, six sisters, a cow and a horse. Music was in her blood and she listened to the arias of Caruso on the Victrola, accepting the fact that she herself couldn't sing a note. But she could play the piano beautifully.The Classics. Her long, slender fingers always seemed to strike the right keys. Her mother suggested one day that she might have actually inherited her talent by way of reincarnation from Mozart, or Chopin himself. On weekends, in her teens, she had worked at the movie theater, providing sound for the images. She earned just seven dollars a week there but would have done it for nothing. In her way, she felt like she had become a part of the new world of filmed entertainment that was then sweeping the country. There was no question the best of life was ahead of her, yet her mother never let her forget her family's past in Russia…

There were four children, none of whom her father could afford. The problem worsened when, in 1903, she burst from her mother's womb. Seeing her very bleak surroundings, she might have wanted to crawl back in. Now, for Sholom, there would be another mouth to feed. Still, despite the family's poverty, he was hopeful and you might say even happy sometimes, when, for example there had been no pogroms for a while in the small village of Lubel, near Kiev, in Russia. At such times, he might even joke that "the Tzar's horses were probably tired and needed a rest."

The house in which the Wurtzman family lived was not pretty. There were three small rooms, a leaky roof and a miserable dirt floor. On the other hand, not everything was bad. At dinner they had dark bread, with vegetables grown on their small plot of land, and fish caught in the Dnieper River nearby. They also had ice cold water to drink. In the hot Summer months, a breeze blew through the door and in the winter a wood stove kept them warm. Of course, the other villagers, most of whom were Jews, were no better off, yet hope prevailed since everyone in the small community, encouraged by the words of their Rabbi each week at the Shul, believed that he or she would see Jerusalem someday.

As the years passed and each child arrived, Sholom's income from selling used clothing at the village market had seemed to decrease. He suspected it might be God's wrath coming down on him for the enjoyment he received from sex with his wife. In any event, matters were getting worse. But since he prayed daily and continued to believe that he was one of God's "chosen people," he was not completely astonished receiving a letter one day from Lina's brother Max who had been living in America for seven years. In the letter were boat tickets to America. Written in Yiddish, Max had explained about the joys of being in America. He was living in a place called "Batavia in Western New York." He had opened a furniture store there, and was doing very well.

"No one bothers me except my wife who is eating too much andgetting too fat… a joke," he noted. Since Sholom was impressed by the tone of the letter, he asked his wife, "Why should we stay here?"

She had no answer.

"Maybe the Cossacks will miss us ?" he offered, after thinking about it. He was always making jokes like that, Lina thought. At such times, the plump, good natured woman would burst into laughter at the absurdity of what her husband had said. The next day, though, a decision was made. They would sell everything and leave Lubel. They would have to hurry.

The boat would depart in only six weeks from the seaport at Antwerp, Belgium bound for America.

Sholem found a buyer for his horse, Schmalka , even though the beat up animal, dangerously close to starving, would have happily agreed to go to America and starve there. But he had never been asked. The very next day, Sholem disposed of his inventory of clothing while Lina gathered together her secret stash of gold coins and some jewelry handed down to her by her mother. It would be used to bribe border guards and pay for the trip to freedom.

Everything they had talked about had happened. Sholom was in America. After several years of hard work in Batavia, New York collecting scrap metal and other junk, his other dreams were coming true. He had bought a horse and wagon and a house with help from Max. The house had a spacious back yard in which he could store the junk when prices were too low and sell it when conditions improved. One day, he noticed the Model T's bouncing around in the dirt and *potholes of the streets . Rubber tires on these and other cars didn't last long and were usually discarded in back yards and along the roads of Batavia. He started collecting tires. Each month the piles grew higher in his back yard until they reached the lower branches of the yard's trees. Henry Ford himself called one day on the phone. He was interested in rubber but had not yet developed his rubber plantations in Brazil at Fordlandia in the wilds of the Amazon. Ford wanted to buy Sholom's tires. Sholom, now calling himself Sam, (although still speaking with the accent he had brought from Russia) accepted the millionaire's offer of $8,000. He put most of the money in the bank. With the rest, he bought his sons Harry, Simon, Al and Benny new shoes with leather soles at the department store. He bought his daughters Libby, Bessie, Edith, Paula, Mary and Fanny each a colorful new dress. And then, like his God, he rested.*

A few weeks later he got another call from the auto magnate.

"I made a mistake," Ford said sheepishly. "I sent you too much money, Mr. Wurtzman. It should have been only $7,000. You'll have to return the difference."

Sam, who had never taken a dime he wasn't entitled to, didn't even question the strange mistake. The next day he went to the bank and sent a check for $1,000 to one of the richest men in America. The children kept their gifts.

Fanny was not the first of her siblings to fall in love, nor the last. In 1927, at a girlfriend's wedding, she met a handsome, Buffalo lawyer. Ben Marsh smiled with a twinkle in his gray blue eyes. He touched her arm and whispered in her ear that she was the most beautiful girl there. They talked for a minute. She blushed because she knew from the way her girl friends giggled that they had overheard him. He got her telephone number. She looked away for a second and when she looked back he was dancing with another girl named Sadie.

She was surprised to hear from him again a week later and she invited him to the house. They sat nervously in the big room with the brown upright piano on which she had learned the finger movements and technique to become a talented pianist. She played the piano for her new suitor. She wanted to impress Ben Marsh. She chose the 'Moonlight Sonata' for its ethereal qualities. He was entranced by the music and by her beauty. He looked at Fanny like there was no one else in the room, although her mother and father and a few of her sisters were there, staring at him with the same intensity as members of one of his juries. Later, when the two of them were alone, Ben told Fanny she looked like Norma Shearer or maybe Gloria Swanson. "I've heard that line before," she said. He kissed her on the cheek . Then he told her about himself....

From the top of the hill where the University of Syracuse Law School resided, Ben Marsh could just about see his family's store. The sign on the building said "Marsh Kosher Meats." Max and Pearl, Ben's parents, like most of their customers, had endured much suffering in Europe and had something else in common too. Their names had all been changed at Ellis Island . Ben had been lucky. He had been born in America. Yet he had always been curious about what his family's name had been in Poland. Marskofski? Marshkewitz? His mother and father had never quite gotten around to telling him and now, as he studied his law books for the Bar exam, he didn't care anymore. Soon, he would be a lawyer and his future was bright. Hadn't Adolph Perry, his law professor, said just that?

Even though he had graduated in the bottom half of his class (a statistical anomaly due to too much time spent after school working as an electrician), he had maintained a quiet confidence about the future. And he had ideas. Professor Perry had once complimented him on his innovative application of the law to real life situations. In his last year at Syracuse, he hadn't forgot the pat on the shoulder. He hadn't told his parents yet, but he was going to move to Buffalo, 150 miles away on Lake Erie. He thought he could do better there in a bigger city. He wanted to make money to pay his mother back and support a family of his own and he was in a big hurry.

For as long as he could remember, his mother, Pearl had spent most of her time in the Butcher shop, worrying about money and her son's future. Max could usually be found in the Shul, praying, confident that God would provide. Pearl hadn't been so sure, especially when their business was slow.

In Buffalo, Ben met Harold Lipsky, an older lawyer who needed help. Ben offered to try his cases in return for office space and a percentage of the fees. Lipsky agreed to the arrangement which turned out to be attractive for both of them. After only a few months, Ben was able to rent a spacious one bedroom apartment and buy a new car from Henry Ford. He had made $500 in RCA Corporation stock and would make much more if President Hoover had anything to do with it.

Our drinks were cold now like the air coming in from under

the door. I pulled my robe around me. My mother adjusted her sweater.

"And then you got married," I said, hoping she'd continue.

"Yes. In 1927," she said. "We were happy. He bought me the black Steinway you see in the living room. Then I had your sister in 1928. Everything was wonderful…at least until the Depression ruined everything…."

When the market crashed, in 1929, the papers said nothing had changed except the bank accounts of a small group of Wall Street bigwigs. Insurance salesmen went to work and children went to school. The A @ P continued to sell food (cheaper than before) and people laughed at the joke about the man who went into a hotel one night for a room and the desk clerk asked whether he wanted it "for sleeping, or for jumping." Suddenly, however, money was scarce. When the banks closed in 1933, things got worse. But FDR said that the nation had "nothing to fear but fear itself." To Lipsky, these were only a bunch of words. He was having trouble paying the rent for his office. Ben was also nervous about supporting his young family. His confidence was shaken. But he was a self starter. Suspecting that crime would increase, he passed out cards at seedy restaurants, tire stores and gas stations, looking for criminal cases. He charged fifty dollars. One hundred if he went to trial. Two clients a week were a living. Double that again and the Marsh family went out for dinner. Then he got a barter deal with farmers outside of Buffalo. Legal services for bushels of apples and Fresh eggs. The harder Ben worked the luckier he got, as the saying goes. He met a man in a barber shop. He promoted himself as the best trial lawyer in Buffalo. The man was impressed. He gave

Ben's business card to an injured friend, Frank Connolly who had lost a leg to a freight train of the Erie RR. His car had stalled on a crossing. When he had tried to open the door of the car it was stuck shut. The train's engineer, seeing Connolly's car on the tracks from a distance, had blown the train's whistle "ten times" as he approached. "Even a deaf man could have heard it," he would say on the stand a year later, "I kept blowing it for two minutes but the car didn't move. What else could I do?" he asked, looking squarely at the jury. "The whistle was screaming, 'Get off the tracks, get off the tracks,' " Ben Marsh said on his summation. With tears, real or feigned in his eyes, the words rushed out of his mouth, reminiscent of Clarence Darrow on a good day. "As the train of the Erie Railroad bore down on my client, Mr. Connolly," he continued in front of the 12 man jury, "neither man nor beast could have got him off those tracks because the door to his car wouldn't open. Yes, Mr. Connolly had something to drink that day. He was broke and lonely, a problem that you or I might have someday. And at times like that, sometimes a bottle of whiskey is the only place to turn. But then, on the tracks, he had suddenly become imprisoned against his will by a trick of fate. He couldn't get out of the car. He wanted to get out , he wanted to live, to reclaim his life, but the train of the Erie Railroad, that giant Corporation with neither heart nor soul, was bearing down on him saying 'Get out of the way. Get out of the way or I'll ram you.' " Before the trial, the Erie Railroad had offered to pay Connolly's bills and a nominal amount, confident of the rightness of their position. After all, they had conclusive proof that Connolly was drunk at the time and had carelessly driven his car onto the track. Ben Marsh, having once been highly praised in law school for having clever interpretations of the law, had invoked the rarely used and almost forgotten legal Doctrine of "Last Clear Chance." Against the objections of the Railroad attorneys, the judge had agreed, after duly researching the subject, to charge the jury exactly as Ben had requested. "Regardless of a plaintiff's own negligence," the judge said looking at the Jury, "if he is physically unable to extricate himself from danger, and if the defendant (RR) had the last clear chance to avoid the accident and didn't act, then ....liability should ensue. Within a half hour, the jury had returned to the courtroom, bringing in a verdict against the Erie for twenty five thousand. It was a lot of money in the Depression. Soon after that, and for the rest of the decade, Benjamin Marsh was telling everyone that he specialized in railroad cases .

Our conversation had ended. We sat quietly, savoring the silence, yet still basking in the past.

"You just sounded like you love him, still," I said.

A tear gathered in her eye. "Yes, I did, didn't I."

Chapter eleven

Going Hollywood

In the year, 1949, several important events occurred almost simultaneously: Albert Einstein propounded a brilliant theory about Gravity which no one understood... I accumulated 100 Superman's and Captain Marvel's in my bedroom closet leaving little room for my clothing and my parents, after twenty three years of marriage, had become strangers again.

Ten years after the Great Depression had ended, my father's law practice had become successful and yet, from my hiding place at the top of the stairs, I gathered that he still didn't believe the "good times" would last. He worried about everything but mostly about money, his health, and a general lack of companionship. (My mother was spending more time talking on the phone with her clubwomen friends than with him.) They slept in separate rooms. We ate dinner in silence. Most of the time, my father retired to his bedroom after dinner to relax alone with the evening paper or the radio.

His frustrations touched us all in varying degrees. My sister, Sybil, a beautiful dark haired girl of nineteen, seemed to be the least affected, influenced more by what boy she was dating than by the constant family discord. Looking for attention, I became a severe annoyance to my father, often running for my life from his leather belt. My experience in fleeing from my grammar school bully, Calvin, had, however, resulted in an unexpected advantage. I was now faster than my father.

As June approached, some things were about to change. I overheard my mother and sister talking excitedly one day in the kitchen about "California." At that time, we had several close relatives living in Los Angeles and one we had never met, a particularly famous relative who was my mother's second cousin, Dore Schary, the soon to be successor to Louis B.Mayer,as head of MGM. None of us mere mortals, including my mother, had ever talked to him but his name seemed to come up every time she reminisced about her Russian roots and how she had crossed the ocean from Europe as a baby. She had assumed he and his family, and hers, had been on the same boat as it crossed the Atlantic in 1903. Years later she discovered that he had, in fact, been born in Newark, New Jersey in 1905. It didn't matter. He was "meeshpucheh,"(a family member) binding them irrevocably (and proudly) together for all time.

Meanwhile, Sybil waited patiently for marriage or some other life transforming miracle to get herself out of the mad house on Summer Road. A screen test at MGM would do. Everyone had always sworn she was pretty enough to be in the movies. Besides, she could play the piano almost as well as my mother and could sing. Now, in the kitchen, Sybil was making mysterious references to Dore Schary again.

"Do you think he'd see me ?" She asked nervously.

"Why not? He's my cousin," my mother said confidently.

I didn't understand what they were talking about (had the Great

Man come to Buffalo?) until later that day when my mother broke the news that we were going to spend the summer in Los Angeles. Without my father. Amazingly, he had said he would remain in Buffalo and pay for the entire trip. Remembering their argument one night about a woman who was paying too much attention to him , I wondered if he might have some nefarious reason for staying behind in Buffalo. My mother must have wondered also. But who cared ? We were to fly out to California in two weeks, soon after I graduated from grammar school. (Goodbye Calvin, hello happiness!) I was excited at the thought of traveling to the fabled land called "Hollywood," wherein resided the movie stars I saw every Saturday afternoon at the Hippodrome. "Holy Geez," I said to myself. (It was my favorite expression.) Someday, my sister might be a star herself. Mother said it was almost a certainty. "Holy Geez, " I thought.

When I told Sally, she was sad I was going, but happy I would see some other parts of the world as she had. It would only be for three months anyway. A few days before I left, I called Hacky. He said, "Have a great trip and say hello to Rin Tin Tin, for me."

At last, the big morning arrived. At seven o'clock, we started for the airport, stuffed into my father's Buick Road Master purchased after he had won an important negligence case against the New York Central RR. In the car, my father and mother didn't speak. At the airport my father kissed my mother lightly on the cheek, and hugged Sybil. He shook my hand and touched my shoulder. Mother cried a little . They had rarely been apart. Soon we were off, strapped tightly into our seats. The giant silver American airlines DC 4, with it's four smoking, propeller driven engines, dragged us swiftly into the morning sky. None of us had ever flown before. There was unstated risk, though the pilot's calm voice was reassuring. I sat next to the window, watching the ground recede until all I saw was a patchwork quilt of farm land and country roads. On Sundays, there had been times when we had driven out to farms below to buy fresh eggs or walk in the fields to pick corn on the cob. Now, as we climbed toward ten thousand feet, I barely thought of the past. Ahead of me lay Los Angeles, Hollywood, the Pacific Ocean, Dennis Morgan, the actor (my secret role model), and the vast MGM studios where there were "more stars than in the Heavens," ...or so they said.

Our first stop was Chicago. We would refuel there and take on supplies. The pilot seemed overly nice, talking slowly, explaining everything like we were in third grade. (Commercial flying was in it's infancy then and the airline Companies were actively trying to take business away from the trains and buses which was the way most people traveled longer distances.)

After Chicago, we would be landing at Dallas' Love field where we could get some refreshments and walk around. Then on to Los Angeles. The whole trip would take about twelve hours, arriving in the movie capital about nine at night.

Not long after getting airborne out of Dallas, I remember being very tired. The monotonous noise of the engines had become somehow comforting. Mother and Sybil were quietly reading magazines when, somewhere over a giant mountain range, I fell asleep and into a dark dream I which Calvin was dragging me like a sack of potatoes along the aisle of the plane toward an open door. I was screaming but no one heard me. A quick thrust of his foot and I was plunging wildly through a rain filled cloud while the earth below rose up to meet me. I awoke with my heart pounding, hearing the heavy wheels of our plane being lowered and it's engines slowing and the pilot saying we were entering Los Angeles airspace. I looked out the window into the early evening's darkness as the plane's left wing over which I was sitting bent sharply downward toward the blanket of lights below. How could the pilot find the airport in the dark or know where to land? My mother didn't seem to care. While I worried, She was talking calmly with my sister about the arrangements she had made with her friend Hedi to pick us up at the airport.

Hedi Golden (formerly "Goldenrod,") had moved to Los Angeles from Buffalo six years before but she and my mother had remained friends, keeping in touch with each other over the years. Her husband, Marvin, capitalizing on a major shift of population into California after the war, had opened and now operated a very successful drug store on Santa Monica Blvd, while Hedi, who had done some minor radio broadcasting in Buffalo, had managed to transform herself into a successful radio talk show host interviewing young aspiring actresses.

Hedi was waiting for us as we got into the terminal. She recognized my mother immediately. Mother, on the other hand, didn't recognize Hedi until she heard her distinctive voice. Her modulated alto was now slightly more modulated, while other parts of her had changed dramatically. Her light brown hair had become a luxuriant fire engine red, flowing outward in several direction much like her hips. "I love to eat at the 'Brown Derby' with all the stars," she bubbled on the way back in her Buick convertible to her home in the Hollywood Hills where we had been invited to stay for a few nights.

Mr. and Mrs. Marvin Golden must have been cashing in on Southern California prosperity, big time, because their house was something out of a magazine, a two story white colonial with an expansive two hundred foot carefully manicured lawn peppered with graceful palms and colored flowers that I had never seen before. Everything rose gently toward God, even the path in the back of the house that led us up into an Eden like flower farm, terminating at a large pool filled with orange fish.

"Do you eat those?" I asked naively. "No darling," she laughed. "They're just for looking."

The next day I woke up and discovered that Hedi had a daughter. She was sitting on the bed and she was nearly the prettiest girl I had ever seen.

"Good morning, Mr. sleepyhead, " she said , giggling a little.

"Hi," I said hesitantly, one eye open. I thought I might be dreaming.

"I'm Sandi. My mother's Hedi. She brought you here last night."

"I know," I said. "I was in the car when she was driving."

She laughed like I had just said something funny.

I was hoping she'd leave the bedroom soon because my heart was pounding and I had to urinate badly, except that I didn't have anything on beneath the covers. I didn't know how to tell her.

"Where's the bathroom?" I asked. Maybe she'd get the idea.

"Around the corner," she said, pointing to the far wall.

"I mean…. uh .. Actually I don't have …. You know…"

"Oh," she said. "You don't wear pajamas." she paused long enough to make me flush. "Either do I," she continued. "No one in our house does…. anyway, I'll leave while you go "pee, pee" as we say here in Hollywood." She giggled and left the room, a little too familiar about my toilet habits, although I'd never tell her that.

That day Hedi and Sandi took us to the Brown Derby for lunch. The only stars in the restaurant were those in the pictures on the finely paneled walls. At Hedi's suggestion, my mother and sister ordered the latest Hollywood creation, the Cobb Salad. I was not especially into that kind of thing and asked for a hamburger and French fries. Sandi ordered the same. Hedi must have felt she had failed us in some way since none of us had quite finished eating when she called the waiter over, asked for the bill and said, "Let's go across the street (Wilshire Blvd.) to the Ambassador Hotel. You can see the famous Coconut Grove Night Club... and who knows who's by the pool on a Sunday afternoon."

At the hotel, none of the stars we knew and loved were anywhere in sight. Where were Gary Cooper, and Errol Flynn and Elizabeth Taylor? Even Lassie would do. I looked for the handsome canine but saw only an inconsequential homely Pekingese carried by a large woman getting into a Rolls Royce. In spite of our disappointment mother had already decided to check in the next day to this monument to historic Hollywood glamour. Early the next morning after breakfast, we arrived at the Ambassador in our rented Hertz automobile, and got settled in our room. Then we invited Hedi and Sandi to spend the day with us. By noon, everyone was in bathing suits and down by the pool. Sandi had on a light green two piece suit most of which clung to her like fly paper and revealed everything I had imagined. By the time we sat down, I had fallen in love at the age of fourteen.

"Well, how do you like Los Angeles?" Sandi asked from a lounge chair a few feet from the biggest pool I had ever seen. I suspected that Esther Williams might appear at any minute smoothly stroking her way from one end to the other while thirty beautiful girls bounced across the water in a Busby Berkeley extravaganza. "Is it much different here than in Buffalo?"

"We don't have palm trees in Buffalo," I said.

She laughed easily. Encouraged, I continued: "and there's a guy in Buffalo who likes to use my head for a punching bag."

She laughed again at the cheap line I had swiped from a

gangster movie I had seen at the Hippodrome, and I didn't even feel guilty about it.

At noon we ordered turkey clubs and iced Coca Cola in tall glasses, served by the pool. The waiter, a blond haired homely guy of about thirty who looked like he hadn't had a date for six years, kept staring at Sandi like she was one of the expensive deserts on the menu.

If there was a paradise, this was it. It was the first time I had ever eaten a club sandwich or even heard of one but I said nothing to show my ignorance of the finer things in life. After a while, Sandi and I moved to other chairs partially shaded from the sun by large green umbrellas. Dark sunglasses covered her eyes. I could see her looking at me. Squinting without sunglasses, I must have looked like Edward G. Robinson just before he had plugged somebody in the chest.

Thirty feet away from us, my mother, sister and Hedi were talking about dress sizes and gall bladders being removed and whether life existed on other planets as Einstein or somebody had said. I mostly wasn't listening since I was trying to concentrate on the next hilarious sentence I could spring from my genius mouth to make Sandi laugh. After a few minutes, with nothing coming out, Sandi yawned and carelessly drew her slender legs up to her mature breasts. I managed to steal a glance at her skimpy suit where it failed to quite meet the inside of her tanned thighs. She was smiling when I looked up.

"I'm up here," she said.

"What?" I said, embarrassed.

"Never mind. So tell me, would you like to live here?"

"I'd love to," I said, recovering fast. "Every time I've seen a movie in Buffalo, I think of how great it would be to live here."

"Maybe you will then," she said.

"We're only here for the summer unless my sister gets into the movies."

She looked over toward Sybil. "She's very pretty, but wouldn't that be a little hard to do? A lot of girls come out here to get in the movies and wind up disappointed."

"My mother's cousin is Dore Schary at MGM."

"Really? Well, I guess that could make a difference."

"Why don't you try to get in the movies?" I said.

"I don't think so. But thanks for thinking I could."

"I'll put in a good word for you when I talk to Dore," I said.

Sandi laughed loudly. "I'm not going to hold my breath."

"Do you date much?" I asked, looking toward the pool, and trying to sound only vaguely interested in her love life.

"I guess so, but guys think they're all God's gift and they expect things."

"Like what?" I prodded.

She smiled. "That's for you to figure out."

Two days later we checked out of the hotel and moved into a three bedroom apartment on Veteran Drive in Westwood Village, a beautiful suburb of Los Angeles. We were at the top of a hill that plunged steeply toward the Village below. The apartment was owned by a Doctor and his wife who spent their summers in Europe. The rent was two hundred fifty a month which Mother had cleared with my father on the phone before doing it. Surprisingly, he didn't object. He must have missed her already. I wasn't sure how my mother felt.

The first order of business in Los Angeles was calling the MGM studios to talk to our cousin. He wasn't in, or so his secretary said. She compounded my mother's disappointment by being insultingly aggressive. "Who are you?" she sneered.

"We're very close relatives from Buffalo. First cousins."

"Mr. Schary is very busy,"she said a little nicer. "He's about to leave for New York for the opening of his new movie 'On the Town'."

"Couldn't I just say hello for a minute?" my mother pleaded.

"Sorry, but If I put you through to him, he'd miss his plane. He's 'taking' dinner tonight in New York with Mr. Frank Sinatra."

"Oh?"

"Call him in a week," Miss Cold heart said. And that was that.

June was now absolutely shot, I figured, as far as Sybil having a screen test and becoming famous and us living in Paradise Found. We picked up the pieces the next day and explored Westwood Village proper. A girl got into a car. It was almost certainly Mona Freeman, a rising young starlet, who lived next door.

"There's Wallace Beery," I hollered the next day at the top of my voice as we cruised down Sunset Blvd. The heavy set man was walking slowly behind a large German Shepherd. As we got closer, we noticed that the man, while having a passing resemblance to Beery, was actually blind. Our need to see movie stars was turning out to be so overwhelming that we were now making up our own reality.

Every day we saw someone that reminded us of the rich and famous. They were all stars we had long idolized in the "sticks" of Buffalo. At the famous Los Angeles Farmer's Market, we had a definite sighting of "the girl next door," June Allyson, whose sweet angelic face could not be duplicated. She stood not far from us, with some friends evaluating tomatoes. None of us had the nerve to ask her for an autograph.

The following day, satiated with our first absolutely genuine star sighting, we spent the day getting some color in our cheeks at Santa Monica Beach. There, bathing in the cold salt water at various times were Clark Gable... Doris Day ...and Bing Crosby...or reasonable copies thereof.

After that, we spent considerable time with the Golden family. One night, after dinner at their home, the adults were downstairs and Sandi and I went upstairs. She wanted to show me some pictures from an album. We sat on the floor of her bedroom with the door closed. She was doing most of the talking but I wasn't hearing much of what she said. I was preoccupied with her very short black shorts and pink tight fitting sweater. Every once in a while she raised her arms above her head, stretching like she was tired. After a while she rose, went to the bathroom, and on the way back settled on the bed against the headboard. "Why don't you sit over here" she invited. "It's more comfortable." From the jackknife angle of her legs on the bed, the edge of her white panties seemed to jump out at me.

I got up from the floor and sat down on the bed a few feet from her. "I guess this is more comfortable," I agreed.

"These are some pictures of us when we lived in Buffalo," she purred softly. I could barely hear her and couldn't see what she was pointing to. I slid over so that my back rested against the headboard, aware of my hips touching hers and my pants being suddenly too tight.

My heart was pounding. Where was this was all going. If I touched her, would she scream? Her parents were downstairs, probably even then (I was sure) listening for the first sounds of a struggle that would signal the attempted deflowering of their only daughter. Then again, what would she think if I did nothing?

That I wasn't interested in her or that I was too scared to act? My mind was full of doubts and contradictions. After almost five minutes of indecision, I managed to summon up enough courage to brush my hand slowly across her knee. Apparently, though, I had waited too long. She shrugged her shoulders, got off the bed and opened the door, ending the sexual tension. I had apparently lost the opportunity of a lifetime. Years later, still regretting my timidity, I cringed at what she must have thought of a boy too shy to grab the "Golden Ring."

A month after we arrived, the three of us, my mother, sister, and I, for the second time, sat at the Brown Derby in an oversized red leather booth, still star struck, trying to look important enough to be sitting amidst the rich and famous surrounding us. That's when Buddy Clark walked in, greeting people to his left and right, obviously more hungry for the adulation of the diners than the Cobb salad the Derby was offering.

My mother had read in a local paper that he was currently singing at the famous Greek Theater. His ultra smooth voice, comparable, many said, to that of Crosby, combined with a beautiful head of hair that made him better looking than Bing, had placed him (with his smash hit song "Linda") at the top of the popular music world.

It was immediately obvious to me that the chances of the famous singer stopping to say hello to three unknown "hicks" from Buffalo was somewhere between 0 and minus 10. I was wrong. When he saw Sybil he did a first class imitation of Douglas McArthur performing a military about face and sat down uninvited at our table.

"I'm Buddy Clark," he said, looking at my sister, "and you're beautiful. Where have you been hiding ?"

"We're from Buffalo," Sybil gushed. "We're here to see our cousin at MGM, Dore Schary."

"That's great. Why don't we talk about your cousin Dore when I take you out sometime? "Of course, with your sister's approval," he said, looking directly at my mother. He winked at both of them and showed his straight white teeth and practiced million dollar smile. His dental bills must have been enormous.

I looked over at my mother.

She was giggling like a fifteen year old school girl.

"Maybe you both can come over and hear me sing sometime at the Greek Theater," he said. "I can leave tickets at the box office. Bring your little brother too," he said, looking at me, almost like we were related.

While I was glad he had included me in the conversation, even as a child, I had always been suspicious of overly friendly people. Besides, I didn't like to be called "little."

He called the next day and showed up at our apartment. He discussed his career without being asked and then enumerated his plans for the evening. "We're going to Ciro's night club," he said. "It's a great place to dance. Then I'll show your daughter some of the sights in Hollywood and have her home before midnight so you don't have to worry."

That night they danced and drank highballs and then later parked on a dark street overlooking the lights of Los Angeles. That was when he showed her the "sights." It wasn't what my sister, a virgin, had exactly expected. She ran screaming from the car before Clark had had a chance to pull his zipper up. Barely managing to get to a phone in the dark, she called a cab and returned to civilization before the Los Angeles sun rose in the morning sky.

Under ordinary circumstances, we would have continued bad mouthing him for years to come, except that fate stepped in a few months later after we had returned to Buffalo. While retuning from a college football game, Clark and several of his friends, flying in a twin engine Cessna, had run out of gas and crashed on Beverly Boulevard in Los Angeles. Everyone survived except Buddy Clark. The papers said that one of the great singers of his generation had died. We were shocked and saddened by it. In his death, we had lost an intimate connection with fame that had separated us from the mundane lives of ordinary people.

In July, in the Los Angeles paper, we noticed that our cousin Dore Schary had returned from New York the week before. He hadn't returned my mother's call. When she called him at the Studio the secretary said he was still very busy and couldn't talk. Mother sarcastically said we were "still very close cousins." She again left our phone number. Another week passed and then another and we wondered if he was getting any of our messages. Finally my mother gave up trying. But we still had California.

In August my mother met "Morry" at a supermarket. He was fifty years old, divorced, a writer at one of the studios. He followed my mother around until she would talk to him. He was tall, funny and not bad looking. He lived in a one room apartment in a very modest section of Hollywood, still waiting, after five years, for the writing credits he thought he deserved.

Mother liked him though. He made her laugh. She gave him our phone number. They went out to restaurants he couldn't afford.

When my mother hinted on the phone about the competition for her heart, my father panicked and took the next flight out to Los Angeles. We picked him up at the airport and drove back to our apartment. He slept on the couch. He was less argumentative than I ever remembered. His sense of humor, once part of their relationship, had returned. He told funny stories, romancing her like he had once done.

When Morry called one day, my father answered.

"Is Fan there?" the hesitant voice asked.

"This is her husband," my father said sternly.

"Oh, I'm sorry I bothered you," Morry said quietly, just before hanging up.

My mother never heard from him again.

As August came to a close, the talk in the apartment shifted to our inevitable departure. A local travel magazine advertised:

"California....where the sun never sets and palm fronds hang gracefully over the shores of the Pacific Ocean, a place where soft breezes bring the smell of orange blossoms to the casual traveler in this fair land."

I was sick at heart leaving the wonderful, crazy, magical glamour of Hollywood, and Sandi's exciting 17 year old sexuality. But what choice did I have anyway? And so one day, joined as a family again, we boarded the giant silver American Airlines plane that would take us back to reality. My father had smoothed over my disappointment by telling me I could, if I wanted, spend my second year in high school at the famous Manlius Military Academy in Syracuse. It was an easy decision to make since I had romanticized for a long time about the idea of a soldier's life, of rising early to the wakeup call of a bugle, of the camaraderie of a group of men on a ten mile march, my rifle in hand, fighting side by side with the likes of Van Johnson in "Battle ground" and Robert Taylor in "Bataan." Exactly what I needed in September of 1949. Or was it?

Chapter twelve

This is the ARMY ?

The dining car of the New York Central jerked violently back and forth through the frigid November early morning air, threatening to jump the tracks at any moment. For an insecure kid of almost fifteen who had run from adversity most of his life, I was strangely unafraid. "Numb" was more like it.

The train, like my life, was heading in the wrong direction, not toward Buffalo, but toward Syracuse and the Manlius Military Academy, where I had been an unhappy cadet for three months.

In late August, barely three months before, I had reluctantly returned with my mother and sister from a summer in the make believe world of sunny California. By then, my father had seen a need to repair his fractured marriage. Wanting time alone with my mother without the distraction I would have inevitably caused, the obvious solution was a military school. Of course, the soldier's life at Manlius had been packaged in such a way as to have a strong appeal for a boy who loved war movies. Still, the hard truth was that my father must have thought it would do me some good. And so, the arrangements had been made.

The train rattled uncertainly on. In Syracuse, I would be picked up by my Aunt and her two sons. They would deposit me on the sprawling campus at Manlius where I had heard "Men were made, not born." What kind of men? I wondered. Men like my father who were so busy with their own emotions that they had little time for their sons?

I stared at the fine white table cloth, more suited to the tastes of a Rockefeller than the grandson of immigrants from Russia and Poland. It made me yearn for the cheap place mats that covered our table at home.

I wanted to pull the lever or whatever it was that would bring the train to a screeching halt. I wanted to turn the train around and go home, even to the dysfunctional home in which I had grown up. But I knew that leaving the school would have entailed a loss of the $1,700 (non refundable) tuition my father had paid. That was definitely out... unless I could somehow convince my mother to convince my father otherwise.

Waiting for me at the school, I knew, would be Robert Rozko, an upper classman who considered me an oaf, unable to adapt to the school's high standards of competence. He had figured me out the second day I had arrived when I wouldn't spit shine his boots. He had decided to make my life a living Hell.

For a while, I had tried to concentrate on my studies. "Knowledge is power," my father had once said and now I was trying to learn all I could under new and difficult circumstances in hopes of making that maxim come true. But Sgt Rozko had a way of disrupting my best efforts to overcome failure.

Among other things, he had a thing about the handling of weapons the school provided for practice at the firing range. He was one of the top sharpshooters at Manlius and disliked anyone who treated weapons with anything but the Godlike reverence they deserved. Cadet Sgt. Rozko , who must have been all of sixteen, had decided I was a danger to not only myself and the other cadets, but also to the entire free world.

The M-1 rifle, our standard issue, you see, was an excellent killing machine to take into battle with you, he sneered, as long as you knew how to load it properly and adjust the sights to maximum usability, which I apparently didn't. He had a way of talking intensely with his eyes darting back and forth that convinced me I'd be going into battle soon against the Communist hoards that would soon overrun America. In my imagination I envisioned escaping to Canada across the Peace Bridge before they had the chance.

Note: The M1 rifle contains a spring activated chamber. It is pried open with the side of a hand, allowing one to insert a cartridge of bullets deep into the chamber with the flick of a thumb. Then one must withdraw one's thumb fast enough to avoid the excruciating pain that occurs naturally when the chamber closes around it .

I laid awake nights suspecting that Rozko had secretly increased the closure speed of my chamber to Mach 3. Each morning, at six AM, I awoke with this suspicion justified, as I confronted the front part of my mangled thumb throbbing to the wake up music of the morning bugle.

Despite my growing fear of pain, I had found a way to prove to myself I wasn't the wimp Rozco thought I was.

Emulating my tough talking Uncle Burt, a star football player at Rutgers in the 1930's, I had decided in late September to play football, despite my size, hoping to toughen up fast. I was 5'4" tall and weighed 104 pounds if you include the permanent swelling that had erupted around my thumb. Trotting onto the field with my artificial shoulders projecting outward from my neck like an emaciated Frankenstein, I confronted Coach , a giant of a man , with the words "Here I am, ready to go." After looking me up and down for a minute, Coach then directed me immediately to the bench area to rest up for the big game the following Saturday.

It wasn't long before I realized I was not cut out to come into direct contact with uncompassionate boys running at me full speed. Fortunately, at practice, I easily eluded them.

Coach , as he watched me go untouched down the field one day, must have seen in his new recruit a speedy receiver in the mold of Jim Thorpe, the legendary Native American athlete. I suddenly envisioned myself as saving the day for dear old Manlius.

On Saturday, the day of the big game, Coach put me in late in the fourth quarter. We were losing by two touchdowns and he was desperate. The ball was hiked and I ran like the wind toward the goal line. The quarterback, an intelligent boy who apparently knew a good thing when he saw it, threw the ball in a high arc directly into my arms just as two boys weighing a combined three hundred pounds converged on me from different directions. The resulting pain in my neck, back and parts of my head made me appreciate, in comparison, the comparatively easy time I had had in Buffalo with Calvin, the bully who enjoyed throwing me to the ground every week after school.

The next day I called my mother on the phone dialing with my remaining operable finger. I had to come home, I pleaded. Otherwise she might never see me again. She would try, she said, but she doubted she could convince my father to reverse the transaction that had put me there . After all, she reminded me, she was still having her own problems with him. I hung up without much hope for the immediate future for either of us.

A week later, she called me with the good news that I could could come home for good in December. I never understood why my father had changed his mind and accepted the loss of money but I did notice when I finally got home that he and my mother were now sleeping in the same bedroom.

Chapter thirteen

A light at the end of the trouble

January, 1950 was electric. It arrived with renewed tensions permeating the house on Summer Road. There were suggestions my father might have acted improperly in the handling of a client's case. Each night, from the top of the stairs, I could hear him and mother speaking loudly about the matter. He was being called to appear in front of the Bar to defend himself in front of the members of the ethics committee. Long after I was supposed to be in bed, I pieced together information I barely understood. Important sounding words , "solicitation… disbarment… Statute of Limitations….flew back and forth across the room like daggers from a comic book assassin. I didn't know what the words meant but my father's voice told me it was too serious to ignore. "I didn't do anything wrong but I'm at the mercy of my clients," he moaned.

She listened, nodding supportively. She had always been sympathetic toward the downtrodden of the world. Her husband had become one of them. She had put aside her anger. They sat

closer together and talked so softly I had to strain to hear them
.

Of course, this did nothing to alleviate my problems with Calvin. Although we were not in grammar school any more, we were now freshmen attending the same high school. Once again, I was fleeing for my life. The old feelings of fear and helplessness regurgitated up through my brain like the bad taste of liver my mother insisted on forcing on me once a week.

Maybe it was because of my father's exhortations to "be a man," or that Eddie at the Deco had told me to stop running, whatever it was, I turned suddenly to confront Calvin racing toward me. My right fist rose to meet his oncoming jaw. A lost moment later, a cheering crowd of my school mates had gathered around me and were patting me on my back. Only then did I realize that Cal was lying at my feet, unconscious.

At dinner that evening, no one, not even my father, could have told me there was no God. In addition to my own sweet moment, my father, with a smile on his face and a glass of Mogen David in his hand, announced that his own problems also had disappeared that day when the Ethics Committee, having heard the evidence, had cleared him of any wrongdoing. He stood up. He had another announcement. He raised his glass in the air.

"Your mother and I have decided something. We're moving to Miami, Florida. Your sister's there and it's time to join her."

After the first flush of excitement, my mind raced back to the year before when Sybil, and her new husband had move to Miami Beach. He had a degree in Journalism from the University of Buffalo but no one in Buffalo or points west had seemed to care very much. With nothing to lose, they had left for Florida in a freezing snowstorm in the winter of 1949.

My father, still standing at the table, continued. "Just think,

Lee. You'll be able to fish from the bridges and pick coconuts right off the trees."

I didn't need any convincing. Before he had gotten past the word "fish", I was already salivating like one of Pavlov's dogs.

But I did have a practical question. It was more curiosity than anything else.

"What are you going to do in Miami, Dad?" I said.

"I'm going into the used car business," he said evenly, as if he were telling me the time of day.

Chapter fourteen

Easy come... easy go

I figured my father didn't know any more about automobiles than I, at fifteen, knew about brain surgery. Yes, he had been driving cars for years. And he could change oil with the best of them. But did that qualify him to own and operate a car lot? On the other hand, these days in which I am old enough to receive Social Security, and am supposed to be wiser each passing year, I sometimes speculate that the excitement and enthusiasm of a new venture can give one the self confidence to overcome any obstacles to success. On the first hand, though, it had never quite worked out that way for my father.

Ever since he had attempted as a young man to carve up a shoulder of lamb at his family's Butcher shop in Syracuse, or taken in his first dollar at the cash register, he had wanted to go into a retail business for himself. But his mother had pushed him toward the law school on the hill. She wanted him to be a professional. But even after he had graduated in 1927 from Syracuse Law and started practicing the noble profession, the unique feeling of exchanging hard cash for a physical commodity remained implanted in his mind. By 1943, he had been able to save up several thousand dollars and had opened a small fur store on Buffalo's Main Street, hiring a woman with some experience in the fur trade to run it. Not one to burn his bridges, though, he had continued practicing law. He knew it was a long shot since his competition was N.L. Kaplan, the largest and most successful furrier in Buffalo.

My mother, and Mrs. Kaplan, as it happens, were very good friends. Both were involved in the arts. The two previous summers we had been invited to the Kaplan's big farm near Buffalo where I had learned to ride a horse, feed their chickens and become aware of what the trappings of real wealth looked like. My father must have noticed also. Mr. Kaplan's business acumen had brought him the success he deserved. Also obvious was the fact that Buffalo, situated on Lake Erie, was one of the coldest cities in the country, ideal for covering one's body with animal skins. The store my father opened was one floor down from street level, an ominous sign which he ignored, but not for long. In less than five months time he had lost most of his savings, closed the store, and quickly retreated to the relative safety of his law office and its low monthly rent.

Seven years later, his compulsion to succeed in business had once again overwhelmed his natural reluctance to lose money. And so, in June of 1950, we were heading South toward "God's Country," as my father, a non believer, now ironically called Florida.

Chapter fifteen

God's country.

There were two of them. Two Miami's. Miami Beach and Miami. In the mind's of new residents like us, each one qualified for the title "paradise." Only a few miles apart, they were separated by causeways of concrete and wood and steel crossing the great and beautiful Biscayne Bay.

Miami Beach, the smaller of the two, encompassed not only Lincoln Road with its fabulous (and expensive) stores, but also Collins Avenue on the Ocean whose residents could brag that every year at least one new hotel had been erected, each one more luxurious than the last .

Across the McArthur causeway was the larger City of Miami. Less flashy than its sister city, it nevertheless had an extravagant, wide open view of the Bay running along Biscayne Blvd. Nearby was Flagler Street running West through Coral Gables and toward the "Sea of grass" known as the Everglades. Flagler Street had been named after Henry Flagler, the wealthy oilman who, without the help of his more famous partner John D. Rockefeller at standard

Oil, had spent millions bringing rail transportation to Miami in the early part of the century.

All this I learned shortly after I had begun my love affair with the "Magic City." It had begun on a humid evening in June of 1950 as my father found himself creeping slowly along Collins Avenue in his overheated Buick Road Master, searching with red rimmed eyes for a hotel. Since neither I nor my mother knew how to drive a car at that time, the burden had fallen on him and him alone. After driving for nearly ten hours without stopping in the final leg of our journey along US 1, his eyes could barely focus. We had left a dreary, overcast Buffalo three days before, staying at motor camps along the way. Then, after crossing the state line between Georgia and Florida, the orange groves and juice stands had suddenly appeared out of nowhere, encouraging us to press forward toward our destination, the land of coconut milk and honey.

At about nine that evening, Mother and I, comfortably ensconced in the back seat of the car, awoke yawning just as we pulled into the parking lot of the small but attractive Dorchester Hotel. The neon sign in front flashed the exciting message : "SALT WATER POOL. $5 A NIGHT. " Whether it was due to extreme fatigue that evening, or the fact that he had managed to accumulate the handsome sum of $ 35,000 as a lawyer in Buffalo, my normally cautious father carelessly checked in without even asking if the room rate as advertised was per room or per person.

We wound up staying a week, during which time money moved from my father's pants pockets as easily as the warm sea water flowed nightly into the Dorchester's pool. That first week, his natural conservatism, instilled in him during the worst of the Depression, had disappeared. We swam under blue skies at the Dorchester pool like "old money." We ate club sandwiches served under broad umbrellas by the blue green pool. As the sun set each evening we dressed and happily trotted off to dinner at "Pickin' Chicken," or Wolfies, often with my sister and Jimmy, her husband who was still trying unsuccessfully to identify a meaningful job in South Florida.

If Jimmy's employment problems were a brutal warning to my father's own aspirations, he didn't seem to notice or choose to question him. At least not until the second week when reality started to set in.

It had to come. Leaving the pleasures of the Dorchester hotel for an ordinary two bedroom apartment without pool on Pennsylvania Avenue was traumatic. (At least it was close to my sister's efficiency apartment, my mother argued.) Shopping at Food Fair, the giant supermarket chain, we started eating at home more often. My father began scanning the Miami Herald for business opportunities while I noticed that my parents were once again getting testy with each other. It was obvious that he was worrying about the transition from lawyer to car dealer.

The solution appeared to us a few nights later over dinner when my father told us he had struck up a conversation with a man on a park bench along Collins Avenue. His name was Frank Sullivan and it turned out that both of them were contemplating how to make each of their lives more certain since neither had a job at the moment. Sullivan had told my father that he had successfully managed a used car lot in Cleveland, Ohio for ten years and had just recently come to Florida for the weather. My father told him he was looking for someone who knew the car business. Sullivan said, "You're looking at that man."

Because he was dressed well, and exuded a confidence of which my father apparently had none at the moment, my father was impressed even though Sullivan admitted to a "slight" drinking problem in his past.

My father had always trusted people who were that forthright with their shortcomings, present or past. In his legal parlance, he considered it an "admission against interest" all of which made Sullivan believable.

They discussed a collaboration right then and there. My father, increasingly anxious to get into the car business offered him, on the spur of the moment, $100 a week to identify an appropriate lot, stock it with used cars, and then manage it with the expertise he had accumulated in Cleveland. Sullivan had accepted immediately with a breath as pure and fresh as a charter member of AA.

Still, my mother had never had much faith in anyone who drank, had drunk, or was drunk, and said so over dinner that night. But the deal had already been sealed with a handshake and an advance of hard cash. A fait accompli.

Chapter sixteen

Cars

It was simple. If you wanted cheap transportation and were slightly naïve in thinking you understood the term "buyer beware," you would stop at the used car lots along N.W. 36th Street, also known to the locals in Miami as "Poor man's automobile row." Without curbs, nothing separated the street from the sand lots doting the landscape. At least there was continuity. In any event, Sullivan had assured my father that this was an excellent place for a freshman used car dealer to start since it was difficult to lose much money when you paid, for example, only two hundred for a car and a buyer then "forked" over as much as four hundred, you could make at least one hundred percent return on your investment, less "minor" expenses for incidentals.

The lot Sullivan decided on for my father's hard earned cash was almost identical to the others on the street. Each one was structured in 100' by 50' rectangles of hot sand sitting on top of the limestone on which Florida had rested for two thousand years since before the time of Christ. (Not that He would have bought a chariot there.) The distinguishing difference between dealers on 36th Street rested with the signs erected above their lots, all designed to entice unwitting buyers to stop in and fondle the merchandise. Each dealer seemed to stress their individual uniqueness. For example, "Reliable Motors" vied for attention with "Quality Cars" which was down the street from "True Value" cars. Each of the signs, by implication, asserted that the other dealers were either thieves or liars.

My father was sure he had topped the others with a politically astute sign, …. HONEST ABE'S AUTOS.......especially if one trusted the president who had ended the Civil War and freed the slaves, some of the descendants of whom might even be potential customers .

In a corner of the lot, an unpainted shack projected to be used for closings, threatened to ignite at any moment in the heat of the day. From a safe distance away, one could notice that it also leaned dangerously to the left like Italy's tower of Pisa. Since it was Hurricane season and WTVJ, Miami's only television station, had recently warned viewers in august of potentially bad weather, my mother wondered whether there might not be a certain danger to my father, not to mention to any innocent customer who wandered in for a bargain. But for one hundred dollars a month, without a lease, a certain amount of complacency remained in order.

Opening day was hot…August hot. So hot that one could fry an omelet on the sand not that anyone would eat it except maybe the snakes and scorpions that periodically crawled out from under the bushes in the back behind the shack.

Ten automobiles recently purchased from other dealers by our astute new manager were lined up in a straight row a few feet from the street like pins in a cheap bowling alley. Each one had gone through reconstructive metallic surgery to make them more presentable to the public. To that end, Sullivan had hired a giant black man named Jesse Brown willing to work for $30 a week doing what he could to fill holes, paint over car rust accumulated in the moist salt air and apply automobile polish to make each pre-owned "beauty "sparkle in the sun.

Meanwhile, in their comfortable air conditioned cabins one thousand feet above, unaware of the sweating earthlings below, commercial airline pilots floated on silver wings for their approaches to the Miami Airport, a short distance away. What could they know of the suffering below? My father knew it from the amount of perspiration staining his white shirt, and from the money he was risking. Yet I had never seen him so excited. He was like a man walking into the gates of Hell, (almost, but not quite as hot, as the sand beneath our feet) to shake the hand of the Devil. Despite only two customers showing up that first day, we went out to dinner that evening at Sherrard's, on Collins avenue and ordered without looking at the prices.

At eight the next morning, a Saturday, "Honest Abe" and I arose early and were on the lot, in the shack, waiting with Sullivan for a customer. Our new manager mostly talked with (or at) my father but occasionally "threw me a bone" and glanced my way. For the first time since I had met him, I noticed a nervous tic around his left eye whenever he made a questionable statement.

"The best time to sell a car," he assured us one day, tic-ing away, "is the early morning before a potential buyer has a chance to clear the cobwebs from his eyes."

From a distance, the ten resuscitated "dogs" Sullivan had purchased from other dealers lay there in the rising sun, sparkling like sleek old Greyhounds waiting to be raced. And that's the way they stayed for the next month, hungry, eating up the non existent profits of Honest Abe's, remaining unsold and untouched by human hands, except for those of Jesse Brown, the only one who seemed to appreciate the beauty of the metal he had polished to perfection.

By September my father had had enough of the sand lot and Sullivan was in danger of losing his weekly paycheck. Sensing the winds of change, his mantra had changed. "This lot is a sinkhole. You've got to go big," he argued passionately to my father. His facial tics had grown more obvious.

"So what have you got in mind?" My father asked.

"There's a beautiful lot on the "Trail," Sullivan said. "Just vacated. A block long. And it's available right now." Tic, tic.

My father perked up like his horse had just come in at Hialeah. "The Trail?" He said out loud. He had heard stories about Automobile Row where all the action was. But it was expensive and he had gone through three thousand already.

"I Don't know," my father said. "How much for the lot?"

"Four hundred a month, but it's got a lot of drive by traffic and it's right next to a Food Fair super market."

"That's a big jump from what I'm paying now, and we'd have to put late model cars on the lot."

"So what. We'll start fresh," Sullivan said, wiping the sweat from his forehead. Tic tic.

"I'll think about it," my father said cautiously.

But two day's later, he had again succumbed to Sullivan's charms and signed a lease for a year, especially after he found out there was a house in the back of the lot, the first floor of which could be used for transactions, and the second floor containing an unoccupied apartment we could live in.

Two weeks later, we crossed the causeway with our clothes stacked in the back of my father's Buick. The rest of our things, including my mother's treasured black Steinway piano came out of storage and were delivered to our new rent free apartment above the lot on S.W. 8th Street. The next day we discovered we weren't the only ones not paying rent.

A family of large German cockroaches had taken a corner of the living room for themselves. Other creatures had invaded the premises also. That evening, as I stepped into my bathtub, a thirsty scorpion attacked my big toe. I jumped away in time.

My father barely noticed the turmoil. He was spending most of his time downstairs on the lot getting his new business in order. A sign, bigger than the one on 36th Street, had been raised between two tall silver metal poles. Twenty late model automobiles of various colors were stretched gloriously across the front of the block long lot. What remained of the "dogs" from 36th Street were hidden in the back of the lot waiting for delivery to the pound, except for the one my father had given me, a 1937 green Pontiac stick shift which I proudly dubbed the Green Hornet.

In September, I started as a junior at Miami Senior High School. I was in good company since it hadn't been that long since Desi Arnez and Veronica Lake had left the school for movie careers in Hollywood.

Soon, from a new acquaintance, I learned about something which would change my life.

Chapter seventeen

AZA

I wondered whether I really belonged there that night. I was sixteen, in a brand new city and had plenty of doubts.

"Great guys," Yale Bender had said about the boys of AZA when I first met him at his father's soda shop the week before. Yale was the pledge master, "the Aleph Moreh," he said, like he was proud of it. So, despite some misgivings, I had agreed to show up at the Jewish Center in Miami, nervous, unsure of myself, and wary of new, untested contacts.

Twenty minutes early, I sat near the door of the small meeting room in case I wanted to make a quick escape. In the back, several boys were laughing, talking about girls, and mostly ignoring me. They didn't know me but I had seen a few of them at Miami High.

After a few minutes, a boy with a mop of black hair, intense eyes, and a square chin that didn't quite fit his face walked in, scanned the room, and sat down at the door. Seeing me, he held out his hand. "I'm Ray Heller , the Sergeant at Arms," he said.

"I'm Lee Marsh," I said, hesitantly.

"Your first meeting, huh?"

"I guess so…yeh," I said. And probably my last, I thought.

He must have sensed my discomfort: "Is that your car outside, the green one?"

I nodded, wondering why he asked. Maybe he wanted to buy "the little beauty," as my father sarcastically had called it when he had given me the ancient Pontiac taken from his lot.

"Well," Ray said, "As a new member, pretty soon you should have plenty of friends here, and they'll all be asking you for rides… with you paying for the gas, the cheap bastards." He laughed so hard I thought his jaw would unhinge. Ray seemed full of himself, yet I liked him. Besides, he was the only one talking to me, so far .

"What does AZA stand for?" I asked, trying to sound interested, even though I already knew the answer since Yale had filled me in at the store over an ice cream soda.

"Aleph Zadek Aleph. Hebrew words," Ray explained.

"You'll know a lot more by next week."

Other boys had walked in while we talked. The room was three quarters full. And hot. Annoying beads of stinging sweat rolled down my back like the advance party of an angry red ant colony on the move. The slowly revolving ceiling fan above threw off mostly innocuous puffs of air.

Ray looked at his watch. It was one minute past eight. The meeting was beginning with the bang of a gavel from the front of the room. Ray moved the back of his chair against the door and folded his arms. "That's Stu Grossman, the President, the Aleph Godol, " he whispered, nodding toward the boy with a thin brown mustache flanked by two other boys. The President tapped his gavel on the desk again. "Okay, let's sing "Up you men," he said. I rose with the rest. Silently, I listened to the words of the club Pep Song...

Up you men and sing to AZA
time will pass and we'll be on our way
as the years go by there will be
happiest of memories."
(Rah, rah, rah)
"Stand and then, we'll sing this song again
all you loyal men
sing the praises of our order,
Sing up you men of AZA.
(Roll over Mabel, it's better on the other side.)

The boys hooted at the sexual innuendo. The President's gavel came down hard against the desk top, demanding order. I wondered who the mysterious "Mabel" was, did she even exist? Maybe not, but I got the general idea. She was Dorothy Lamour and Veronica Lake and Betty Grable and every other girl I had fantasized about in front of the big Hippodrome theater's movie screen in Buffalo, New York. "Mabel" could also be Sally Pearl who had first taught me to kiss. I remembered how, two years before, Sally had let me look under her dress, a sight that had been magic to my young eyes. Somehow, that image was still fresh, embedded, like nails, in my perverted brain.

The meeting went fast. Motions were followed by short, sometimes angry discussions. I had never heard anything like this before, boys challenging boys with words, not fists. When the noise level got too high, Ray Heller stepped in (backed up by Stu) to warn the group to "keep it down." Ray was not much older than me, though he could have passed for nineteen or twenty.

He sat there guarding the door, sometimes getting up, looking formidably bigger than his 140 pounds. In the early minutes of our friendship, I got the impression he wouldn't take any "crap" …from anybody.

Stu again pounded his gavel on the desk. The room got quiet. He had done his job, moving the meeting forward to its weekly conclusion. He stroked his mustache, looking at the papers on the desk for a minute or so to see if he had forgotten anything. "Okay, we'll have 'Good and Welfare' now, " he said. This was a time, I learned, when members you could talk about anything, except maybe your Aunt Millie's cooking, in which case you would probably be hollered down.

One by one, each boy choosing to speak stood up when prompted by Stu and said his piece. It was mostly fluff.

A heavy set boy named "Yutch" rose . He looked like he could have lifted weights with his teeth. He spoke nervously, without conviction. "I think the meetings should start a little later, at eight thirty, so everyone's got a chance to get in." He looked like he might have wanted to say something more substantive but hesitated a second too long.

"We voted on that motion two months ago, Yutch, and you lost," Stu said.

Yutch sat down with a shrug, as if he didn't really care.

"Harry," Stu said, pointing to a neat looking boy wearing a white shirt and tie who rose and spoke intelligently, and boringly, for three minutes about "Robert's Rules of Order" until somebody yawned loudly. Harry took the cue, rushed the speech and sat down.

Next in line was "Teddy" who told an off color joke poorly. I had trouble getting it. I laughed louder than the others anyway.

After that, several boys waived off Stu's invitation to speak.

But not Yale Bender. He rose slowly, putting one foot on the seat of the metal chair in front of him. Looking around, he said nothing for several seconds. The room was quiet. He stood there, sleek, darkly tanned from weekends at Fourteenth Street beach, looking like Rudolph Valentino in an old silent film .

"Since last week's meeting, I know you've all become excited about the membership drive." His words dripped with sarcasm. Someone in the back grunted like an animal in heat. Yale continued undaunted. "Okay, I know you shits have other things to do," he said, "like playing with yourselves in the bathroom. Just don't shake my hand afterward." Several boys stifled laughter and slumped deeper into their seats. "Look," he said seriously, "I really need some help on this." He stared into a sea of blank faces, their glazed over eyes focused strategically on the barely moving ceiling fan. Yale looked around. Disgusted, he threw his hands in the air. "Okay. Screw it. But remember, it's your club too," he said, sitting down.

"Your turn, Marty ," Stu said without comment.

Marty Safrin stood up with a disrespectful grin on his face. His long sleeved shirt was rolled up to his elbows. He was about my height and weight. His dark brown hair, whether intentionally or otherwise, hung across his forehead like Hitler. I expected him to raise his arm toward the ceiling and salute. "He thinks he's the club's comedian, " Ray whispered.

"Mr. President," Marty said slowly, milking each word. "Mr Sergeant at Arms, Mr. Pledge Master and fellow slobs." Everyone laughed . He was starting to sound like Milton Berle on the Texaco Star theater. Maybe this was what everyone wanted at the meetings . Not any talk of membership drives, or Robert's Rules, but what they got from Uncle Miltie, aka Marty. "All I have to say," he continued, "is that I'm looking forward to the

Sweetheart Dance next month and that I'm taking Linda Rosen, so she's unavailable." The grin on his face got wider . "But she's got a girl friend for one of you guys who can't get a date … if you're interested. And if you're not, there's always "Esperanza." Everyone screamed wildly for a minute until Stu pounded his gavel hard and Marty sat down.

I wondered Who "Esperanza" was …and if she was any more real than "Mabel."

It was Ray's turn. "A few things bother me," he said right off. "First of all, our 'Sweetheart' will be here next week. So let's keep the language clean when she's here, unlike last time." A few guys in the back of the room yawned loudly.

"Yes sir, your honor, " a low voice said.

Ray's eyes narrowed into dangerous little slits. "All right, jerkos," Ray continued with an edge in his voice. "Let's talk about something else. The mess you leave on the floor every meeting." He waived his hand in a dramatic sweep of the anticipated evening's trash. "If you don't clean it up and I have to do it like I did last week, I'm gonna start fining you."

Boos sounded. Spitballs flew.

"Come on, guys. Ray's right," Stu pleaded. "Let's keep the place clean or they'll throw us out of here on our asses."

"Look," Ray continued. The pitch of his voice had dropped a notch. "I'm just doing the job you elected me for, Sergeant at Arms. …"

"Can we have another vote on that?" a falsetto voice hollered in the back.

"You're out of order," Stu said loudly , whacking his gavel.

"Another thing," Ray said, "My chair goes against the door at exactly eight . No one gets in unless he's got a damned good excuse. Like your Grandfather just died, or you lost your virginity to Esperanza." A few giggles.

"Why eight?"

"Because that's what's been decided by a vote. Besides, I read a book that says you're going to grow up to be bums unless you learn to follow authority, and I'm the 'cop' at the door for an hour or so each week."

There were more "boos" as Ray sat down but I could tell from the slight curl of his mouth that he figured he had won the "debate."

For my part, I felt a strange derivative excitement from Ray's words that I had never felt before. I wanted to get up and talk just like that, defending myself about anything, about everything. I was suddenly angry at myself.

A bitter unresolved memory from Buffalo licked at my brain. My eighth grade teacher, Miss Lemke had tried to squelch my passion for writing and I had done nothing at the time to stop her. I had just finished reciting an Americanism essay I had written when she had pounced :

"Did your mother help you write that, Mr. Marsh?"

"No," I said, suddenly embarrassed and confused.

"Why are you lying? " she said coldly.

"I'm not," I said, my voice cracking. I wanted to fight back, to tell her she was the liar but I was paralyzed.

Her lips had seemed to quiver as she had gone in for the kill. "Why are you denying it?" she said. Her eyes held mine in a hypnotic cobra like grip."Just tell us the truth?" her voice cracked, like a bull whip.

I couldn't speak. I heard a few nervous sounds around me from the jury of my peers, an exaggerated cough, a muffled laugh as some of my class mates clearly enjoyed the onslaught not directed at them this time. I looked over at my friends, Hacky and Sally on the other side of the room. Their mouths were open as if they wanted to come to my defense. I sank into my seat, mortified, without a rebuttal, unable to answer her charge, false as it was. The next day, I told my mother about the incident. She had been furious and called the school. The rest of the year, until graduation, my teacher barely glanced at me or asked me any questions...

Back to the AZA meeting.

Stu, was the last to speak, talking about the importance of the paper drive to raise money for Miami 's Homeless. Other than that, he sounded like he was in a hurry to take a pee. For a few seconds he welcomed me, as president, to the club. Everyone clapped and Stu asked for a motion to adjourn, got a second and the meeting was over. He yelled out one last word, "Wolfies" and there was a strange rush for the door. I soon found out from Ray that bad feelings in the meetings would usually dissipate afterward and then we'd all go out to a restaurant to eat and laugh at ourselves playing grown ups.

Usually it would be to the Royal Castle for hamburgers and birch beer. Tonight, we were going to cross the McArthur causeway and head for "Wolfies," the landmark restaurant on Miami Beach named after Wolfie Cohen. There, the rolls and pickles were always free and, if you were smart, all you had to do was buy a cup of coffee, and usually not even that...or so Ray said.

Chapter eighteen

A song to remember

I was born into a musical family. My mother played the piano from early childhood on, almost before she could walk. As a teenager, my sister followed in her footsteps, but her interest in the piano slackened off somewhat as she became a woman. Meanwhile my father played the violin as a young man, thought he was Jasha Heifitz or Fritz Kreisler for a while, (which nobody agreed with) then decided there was no money in it and put the instrument in a closet from which it never emerged. As for me, I started singing when I was eight….the following:

Once I was happy and now I'm forlorn,
like an old cat that is tattered and torn.
My true love has left me and now I'm alone,
the man on the flying trapeze.

Applauding loudly, the members of my fifth grade class had given me in one stroke the encouragement and confidence I needed to take another step forward.

Somewhere between the seventh grade and my so called Bar Mitzvah when I became a man, my high voice had starting changing into a lower register. Not satisfied, I remember longing for the even deeper sounds of Ezio Pinza. Opera was popular in the late 40's and I had by then decided on my future calling. I would become an opera singer. Pinza was on my mind and for weeks, I tried unsuccessfully to lower my voice to resemble the great basso profundo but my efforts only served to produce annoying irritation in my throat which scared me, but not for long.

In late 1950, now in Miami and impatient to make it to the big time, I went to the TV studios of WTVJ for an open talent contest. With legs shaking in front of the estimated 100,000 viewers (including some of my AZA brothers) watching that day on their recently purchased TV sets, I sang "Old Man River." Unfortunately, things went poorly when the woman at the piano (mistaking me for Metropolitan Opera tenor Jan Pierce) began in the wrong key. Thrown into a cold sweat, I was forced to struggle through Jerome Kern's masterpiece two levels above my range. The words of the song seemed to reflect my own frustration:

"Ah gets weary and sick of tryin',
A'm tired of livin' and feared of dyin'
But ol' man river , he jes' keeps rollin' along."

Distraught, I moped around at home for a while thinking of alternative vocations ... possibly selling furniture like my Uncle Burt in California. Then, over dinner one night, my mother came to my rescue, announcing that she had found a singing teacher for me.

Her name was Netta Symes Morris. A onetime opera singer

with the Royal Opera House in London, Ms. Morris had a studio on Biscayne Blvd, not far from the very spot, she said, where seventeen years earlier, in 1933, Franklin Delano Roosevelt, the President-Elect, had almost been assassinated while giving a speech. After that, every time I left her studio after a lesson, I developed a bad habit of scanning the area for dangerous looking characters. I was very impressionable at sixteen.

My new singing teacher, I discovered, was a close friend of Manna Zucca, the famous composer, and Caesar La Monica, the conductor of the Bayfront Park band shell evening concerts. Some of Ms. Morris's students had actually sung for La Monica at the band shell which gave all of us in her class some reason to hope we might have, some day, the same opportunity.

My lessons with Ms. Morris were held on Tuesdays after school. She always sat up very straight in the piano chair in front of her baby grand piano, each time wearing a colorful dress bordered with lace. She must have been sixty five at the time, neither thin nor heavy, wearing blush that made her look younger than her age, yet not quite covering the lines of aging around her eyes and neck. Her soft, friendly smile made that irrelevant.

As a pianist, her skills were not quite equal to her still beautiful voice. My weekly lesson was comprised of singing the scales after which she would patiently teach me a new song or aria, first singing parts of it herself with a flourish reminiscent of her own long ago experiences in England at the opera house.

One day, she surprised me : "Would you like to make some money singing ? She asked.

"Sure," I said, thanking her. The sooner I got some experience the better. Besides, the extra money wouldn't hurt.

She explained: "A few of the hotels on Miami Beach are looking for singers to entertain their patrons and I thought of you.

They want someone to sing mostly ballads and you do that very well. If you want to, you can be at the National Hotel on Collins this Friday night around seven thirty. The manager is a friend of mine and he'll pay you as soon as you finish."

Wearing my dark blue sport jacket, which happened to be my only sport jacket, I managed to time my arrival at the hotel on Collins Avenue for a few minutes to seven. As a newly minted paid "professional" I wanted to look good and be on time. Possibly they would ask me back for a repeat performance and then the word would spread across the Beach. That's how Mario Lanza started, wasn't it? Of course this wasn't the first job I had ever had but it would definitely be the finest. Eventually, I thought, I could quit my job on Saturdays at Food Fair on S.W. 8th Street where I worked as a bag boy tossing meaningless packages of food into paper bags.

As I entered the hotel that evening, it seemed that everyone in the crowd of fifty or sixty people in the main room of the hotel was Jewish. Familiar accents and equally familiar residual smells of matzo ball soup and lox seemed to permeate the room. I was sure Mrs. Buongiorno, the piano player who hadn't arrived yet, would probably feel out of place but that was her problem. A few minutes later, the manager told me she had just called and said she had a flat tire on her car and couldn't make it.

Now it was up to me to impress the crowd, a cappella, for an hour, and hopefully Ms. Morris when the word got back to her.

I waited until the noise in the room died down, introduced myself, then announced the bad news. I would be singing alone. I heard a few whispers of annoyance from the audience and decided on the spur of the moment to begin with a classical piece that I had recently learned.

Out of the night that covers me, (I sang)
Black as the pit from pole to pole.
I thank whatever God's may be
for my unconquerable soul.

Light, disturbing applause followed. Apparently, I had badly misjudged my audience. They had wanted Yiddish songs and I had given them "Invictus." I followed up uncomfortably with popular ballads which I had endlessly rehearsed to perfection with my mother on her Steinway and with Ms. Morris at the studio.

Several seconds after I had stopped singing, the audience became aware of that fact... at which time I heard several yawns, a few claps, and an unnerving screeching sound emanating from someone's defective hearing aid. The manager then rushed up, smiled weakly, shook my hand and handed me an envelope containing five brand new one dollar bills. It was almost enough to pay for my gas and my severely deflated ego.

Chapter nineteen

Getting Miami High

In the fall everyone talked football. Ray Heller, now my best friend, had a strong opinion about Miami High's team, the Stingarees. "We're the guy's to beat," he bragged one day to Yale and me over a greasy hamburger at Mary's restaurant near the school..."A lot better than Edison, Jackson or Beach High. Don't quote me on this but I think we could even beat the University of Miami Hurricanes if we played them."

"It'll never happen," Yale said. "Anyway, how can you compare a high school team to a college team? You're crazy."

"Like a fox," Ray said. "I'd put fifty bucks on us."

"It'll never happen," Yale repeated. "Besides you don't have fifty bucks."

"There's a game Friday night at the Orange Bowl. We're playing Beach High . You wanta go?" He looked at Yale.

"I can't," Yale said. "I finally got a date with Bonnie Berg and I 'vanta be alone,' he said in a falsetto that sounded nothing like Greta Garbo . .... We're gonna hide out at the Olympia theater, in the balcony."

"Bonnie Berg? Miss Iceberg? She's colder than a witches tit."

"Maybe I can warm her up," Yale said with a wink. "She didn't act very cold when I talked to her the other day in class. She squeezed my hand so hard she nearly broke my little finger."

"She's probably going to break something else, like your wiener. I heard she kicked Teddy Soloway in the balls last month when he pulled up her dress."

"I'll let you know what gets broken. Probably her hymen."

Ray waived him off and turned to me. "What about you, Lee? Do you want to go to the football game?"

"What time?"

"Seven thirty. I'm taking a girl. Can you get a date?"

"I don't think so," I admitted. After only three weeks I didn't know any girls I had the nerve to ask.

"I know someone," Ray offered. "Her name's Judy. She's a friend of Carol, my date. Judy likes football and she wants to go to the game but doesn't have a date either. Can I ask her for you?"

"Yeh, as long as she doesn't try anything on the first date," I joked.

"Don't worry, I'll make sure she knows you're a virgin," he said, laughing.

"I'll pick you up in my car," I said, happy to contribute.

Friday was here. My '37 Pontiac was in good condition and would continue to run, according to my father, as long as I put gas in. Still, each time I started it, I wondered if the motor might explode at any time, or the fenders might wind up in the street. That, despite my diligent application of "filler" and Scotch Tape cleverly concealing the metal body under dark green house paint. My mother, upon seeing my handiwork, said the automobile reminded her of an alligator about to attack pedestrians on the street. I wasn't offended, and after I learned how to operate the gears activated by the three foot long floor stick shift which looked to me like an Indian Cobra slithering up from the desert, I became a little more confident driving the car and actually sort of proud of the old crate.

When I pulled up to the curb, Judy and Carol were waiting there with Ray. Judy smiled at me like we were old friends and I said "hi" and didn't have much else to say since my mind went blank. Not that she was beautiful or anything, except that I noticed she had this bright red lipstick on her lips which made me think of Joan Leslie, the movie star, on whom I had a crush for years. Judy kept smiling and showing off her teeth and I thought she must have had her braces removed recently. I was very judgmental about those things. I glanced at her figure and noticed that she wasn't exactly the thin type, not Dorothy Lamour in a sarong or Sally Pearl. But all in all, I had to admit, she wasn't that bad looking either, especially when I saw her sideways, although not as good looking as Carol who had a tight pink sweater on that made her breasts stick out like two Dixie cups. Anyway, we all got in my car and Ray immediately dubbed it the "Green Hornet." Judy got in the front seat next to the stick shift with her left leg almost touching it.

I headed down Flagler Street toward the Orange Bowl. In the rear view mirror, I saw that Ray was tickling Carol. She was giggling, pretending to resist a little but not that much. I watched her breasts bounce up and down, wondering what they looked like without the sweater on. I struck the curb twice but Judy apparently didn't notice as she kept looking straight ahead like she had a stiff neck. Maybe she was as nervous as I.

I was uncomfortable and felt like a dunce not having anything to say to Judy. I admired Ray for that reason. He liked to talk and always said whatever came to his mind, while I had always held back, mostly keeping my thoughts private, still unsure of myself at 16. Usually I would ask questions and listen more than anything else, except now, I couldn't think of any questions to ask as I sat across the seat from Judy.

I played with the floor shift as if I was adjusting it just right, hoping she would ask me what I was doing.

Instead she said, "What are your hobbies?" And I thought: Thank God for her mother who must have coached her before she left about being interested in other people.

"I write stories sometimes," I said, like I had practiced it.

"Really?" Judy asked, her voice rising two octaves, along with my spirits. She smiled and clapped her hands together, like she had just gotten an "A" in Algebra.

Ray heard me and stopped tickling Carol. "You write? About what?"

"A lot of things," I said, feeling suddenly more talkative.

"Like what?" Carol asked.

"Well, a while back, I wrote a story called Mother Mahani's Cookies." (This was an obvious adjustment on the title of my first story, Mother Mahony's Meatballs, a gem of childhood alliteration.)

"Cookies? Is it a food story?" Ray said, sounding a little disappointed.

"Sort of," I said, "but not really."

"It doesn't matter," Judy said, clapping her hands again.

"How does it go?" Carol said.

"You really want to hear it?" I said.

"Tell us, tell us," Judy pleaded.

"Go for it," Ray said.

"Okay, but I only memorized part of it," I said, slowing the car to a crawl so I could think:

"There was …something in the cookies. Tara, girl detective, was sure of it…as she pushed her tiny feet through the foaming surf of the island in the Pacific called Kokoa."

I hesitated only long enough to see if anyone was gagging.

"Go on," Judy said, wiggling in the seat. "I love South Sea stories."

"Go on," Carol said in the mirror like she was really interested. I was sorry her breasts had stopped bouncing.

"Okay," I said, gaining confidence:

"Lately, all the boys and girls on the tiny island were very happy…all except Tara. They laughed all the time. About everything. How the old man, Tahani walked funny. How fish would jump from the ocean. Things like that. They laughed like that only after they took a bite of Mother Mahani's cookies , and Tara was going to find out why…"

We were nearing the Orange Bowl .

"I love it," Judy said, clapping her hands again. "It's like a real mystery. Is there any more?"

"I have the rest at home," I said. "I'll let you read it sometime."

Then we all went to the football game to watch our team wipe the floor with Miami Beach High. Except that it was a tie,

7 to 7.

Chapter twenty

Something on our minds.

The AZA meeting broke up early that Tuesday night. I couldn't remember an evening when the usual "combatants" had argued less about Robert's rules of order, or "good and welfare." Even Ray, the club's best debater and speaker was unusually brief in his remarks. It was obvious that he, and the man with the gavel, Stu, our president, were in a hurry to leave the Jewish Center as quickly as possible, and for good reasons, of which I was somewhat aware. As Ray's best friend, and thus a member of the "inner circle" of the club, I usually went along with him and the others about most things, even matters that might involve potential trouble as they did on this particular night in October of 1951.

Ray and I walked to my car. Yale rushed out as we were leaving and hollered for us to give him a lift. I stopped and he ran over and jumped in the back seat of my coupe.

The window was open and the air was warm outside. Rain had fallen and the damp streets accentuated the sweet smells of Florida's rotting vegetation and night blooming Jasmine which I had grown to love so much .

"Where we going ?" Yale asked .

"You know where," Ray said with an edge in his voice. "The Tamiami Hotel, but only if you fork over 25c for the gas. The Green Hornet doesn't run on air, " Ray said, handing me his quarter. Yale gave me two dimes, a nickel and a wad of fuzz from his pocket.

"What's there ?" Yale asked innocently, as if he didn't know that the Hotel had a reputation as the sleaziest place in town .

"We'll see," Ray said. "Marty wasn't at the meeting tonight because he heard there was something interesting going on there. Maybe a few girls running around naked or something. We're supposed to meet him outside the Hotel near the front."

I stopped at a Texaco station on S.W. 12th Avenue. The sign said "Gas.. 19 cents a gallon." The attendant put in four gallons, and I got onto Flagler street with reckless thoughts of loose women flooding my mind. I drove unevenly toward the corner of Sadom and Gamorrah while Yale caught the spirit of the moment and started singing "Carolina in the morning," with slightly different words that coincided with our mood:

"Nothing could be finer than to be in your v....a , in the morning,

Nothing could be sweeter than to have you hold my p...r, in the morning..."

The three of us laughed in the nervous way that only teenage boys will do in mocking the act of sex about which we all constantly fantasized.

"Where's this place ?" I interrupted.

"On the left. Over there," Ray said, pointing to a rust brown building about two hundred feet ahead. Although I had heard about the hotel's reputation and must have passed it at least three or four times before on the way to Bay front Park, I had never actually noticed the rundown two story structure built over 30 years ago when Miami was young. As we got closer, the building's neon sign was barely decipherable.

"Hot__ Tami ___" the sign flashed suggestively.

Below the sign was a poorly lighted entrance, and a sailor in a white uniform. Both he and the half empty bottle of wine in his hand were tilting to "port."

We parked on the street and walked toward the entrance when we heard Marty call out to us from around the far corner. Several of our AZA brothers were waiting.

"What's up?" Ray said.

"I talked to 'Sailor Joe' over there,"Marty said. "He 's got a girl on the 2nd floor who'll take us on for a buck a piece."

"A dollar a piece?" Ray asked. "What's she look like, Mrs. Bella Lagosi?"

"I didn't see her. So what do you care? We'll put a bag over her head if we have to and pump for Old Glory," Marty said, throwing a mock salute off his forehead into the air.

The sailor stood "at ease" in a drunk sort of way as Marty walked over to him. A dirty hand which had probably been in places I could only imagine was offered and disregarded by Marty. "We've got seven guys here. How is she going to take us all on?"

"One at a time," the sailor slurred, almost stumbling. "She's my girlfriend. Very pretty."

From three feet away, I caught a whiff of 90 % proof rotgut whiskey.

"Is she clean? "Marty asked.

"She took a bath last night," the sailor said seriously.

"So what do we do now?" Marty asked him.

"You pay me here and I'll take you upstairs to the room."

Marty turned to us. "Are we all in? "

A few of us shrugged.

"I'll take that as a yes. Give me a buck each."

Everyone pulled a dollar out of their pants. Marty collected the cash and handed the money to the sailor .

What was I getting myself into, I wondered. My father had told me about disease…. "VD, Syphilis, and Gonorrhea" were the names he had mentioned, for starters.

"Okay. Follow me," the sailor said, wheeling around, almost tripping on his own dirty white shoes.

We entered the hotel lobby and slid past a snoring desk clerk, an old man with white hair. We melded nervously together, climbing a rickety staircase to the second floor. At the end of a long hall was a room with its door slightly ajar. The sailor opened it to display his treasure. I moved a little closer for a better view.

"There she is, boys," the sailor slurred, sounding like a pig farmer pointing to his prized sow .

Over his slumping shoulder, I saw a naked woman with dirty blond hair and too much lipstick on her lips. She was so thin her body seemed to disappear into the folds of the soiled sheets on which she lay. A cigarette hung from her hand which itself hung off the side of the bed. In the subdued lighting of the room, I guessed she was somewhere between forty and fifty.

Others must have been here before us, I thought, maybe the entire Air National Guard unit stationed at Opa Locka. Near the bed, a small table held what looked like a half empty bottle of whiskey and an ashtray full of cigarette butts.

The girl raised herself on an elbow, coughing several times.

She put out the cigarette in the tray and looked back at us blankly, in total submission, it seemed, to the events that had shaped her life, and still were doing so.

"I'll go first," Marty said, pushing to the front, apparently hornier than the rest of us.

"You got a rubber?" Ray asked him. "You better put one on. She doesn't look very clean."

"You think so?" Marty mocked him. He patted his pocket. He went in, closed the door while we waited outside.

"Have you guys got rubbers?" Ray said, to the others.

"I've got one," big Yutch said.

"You don't need one," said Teddy Soloway. "My father's a doctor and he says they can cure anything these days."

"I think she's probably got VD," Ray countered, "I wouldn't do it without a rubber. I'm not sure I want to do it with one either," he said, having second thoughts.

Yale looked at Ray. "Me neither. I've got a rubber but after seeing her, I'm pretty sure you can get something if she just coughs on you."

"But my father told me…, Teddy said.

"I don't care what your father says," Ray interrupted.

I remained quiet, having already secretly decided after hearing the informed discussion of experts present to leave with my virginity and current excellent health in tact.

Stu, hanging back suspiciously from the group, had apparently come to that conclusion also.

"It's too bad we already gave him our dollars," Yale said.

"We should have thought of that before," I pointed out.

While we debated, the four of us were letting ourselves be jostled to the back of the line while Teddy moved to the front.

"Let's get out of here, "Ray said, looking back. Stu agreed.

"It'd be sloppy seconds, thirds and fourths, anyway," he said.

We nodded our agreement, walking toward and then down the ancient wooden stairs, two steps at a time, and out past the still unconscious desk clerk. At the curb, we stood quietly for a minute assessing what went wrong or maybe, more aptly, what we had done right that night. As for me…I knew instinctively there would be a better time to cross the "great divide."

Chapter twenty one
What is this thing called love?

My father smiled down at me from where he stood at the foot of my bed. A sheepish grin covered his face. "I'm traveling to Valdosta today. The auctions. Do you want to come along?"

The offer was unexpected because we hadn't talked to each other in two days ever since he had slapped me on the face in anger over some stupid thing I had done. It wasn't the first time. I had always aggravated him in one way or another to get his attention, and I was still doing so even as my seventeenth birthday approached.

"I'm leaving at nine if you're interested."

I caught a glimpse of the clock beside my bed. It was six in the morning and a good night's sleep hadn't changed how I felt toward him that morning.

"Look, I'm sorry about what happened," he said.

From the way he said it, I knew he regretted what he had done. I shrugged and he touched me on my arm. I felt my anger melting away like an ice cream cone on a hot Miami day and I reached out to shake his extended hand, remembering the last time, four years ago, when we had taken a trip together. The two of us had "escaped" to a little second class fishing camp near Port Colburn in Ontario, Canada, not far from Buffalo, where we slept in a small room with a creaky bed and broken lock on the door. Waking up in the morning, having survived the ordeal, we laughed all through breakfast, then climbed into a row boat with a can of worms and two borrowed poles. Three fish later, (only slightly bigger than the bait) I had grown closer to my father than I had been in years.

The more I thought about it, the more I was looking forward to the trip to Georgia. My father had been at the auctions in Valdosta only once before in the year and a half since he had entered the used car business but he had returned excited about his two purchases. The 1948 Chevrolet and the older English MG convertible (which roared like a speedboat) had both been sold for a good profit. And now he was trying his luck once again. But this time with me.

After breakfast, I was surprised to learn we wouldn't be traveling alone, but with Ralph Hanna, a sixty year old wealthy Miami car dealer. I was disappointed but still felt an overriding sense of adventure developing, similar to the experience I had had in Port Colburn.

At nine, I grabbed my suitcase, kissed my mother goodbye and jumped into the back seat of Hanna's Cadillac, squeezed tightly between Hanna and my father, like a canned sardine. In the driver's seat, with his head almost touching the inside of the car's roof, was a middle age man with a blond brush cut and a day old beard.

His name was Gary and he worked for Hanna. He pulled the car efficiently into the early morning traffic on S.W. Eighth Street, quickly taking us over to US 1 heading North toward

Jacksonville. Hanna told us we would be stopping a few times along the way to relieve ourselves and for coffee and donuts. Once we got to Jacksonville , we'd stop for something to eat at the Mayflower Hotel, and finally proceed on to Valdosta. All in all, It was an eight hour trip to Jacksonville, Hanna said, "depending on the weather."

In the early fifties, before the great super highways of I 95 and the Florida Turnpike existed, U.S. 1, was mostly a narrow two lane road, periodically merging with and decoupling from the old Dixie Highway. Around Fort Lauderdale, 26 miles from Miami, rain started pounding on the windshield. We closed the windows which made the car (without an air conditioner) uncomfortably warm. Despite the storm outside, our car was traveling around sixty and I thought of asking Gary to slow down, but it wasn't my place to do so. Near West Palm Beach, the weather deteriorated and I was increasingly nervous because we were now going seventy and I had trouble seeing anything past the windshield. How could Gary? But my father and Hanna seemed totally unconcerned, talking politics, the Korean War and the merits of Harry Truman as President of the United States.

Each time we skidded dangerously, then rushed wildly ahead, my imagination ran wild, convincing me that the man at the wheel might be a distant cousin of Calvin, my dangerous classmate from Buffalo, secretly sent here to finish the job Calvin had started on me. Everything suddenly fit like a glove: Gary's irreverence for human life, his well practiced ability to stay on the road at high speeds as he must have learned to do on the New York State thruway, his careful glances in the rear view mirror with his cold blue eyes looking directly at me.

As we shot through Vero Beach, unyielding to the elements, I was sure the two of them had conspired to track me down and see to it that I would die this day on US 1. Around the time Truman was being recommended in the back seat for the Nobel Prize, I began to sweat profusely. I knew I'd never live to see him get the award. But shortly, the weather cleared, I saw some blue sky, reason returned, and Gary had become, once again, just Hanna's innocuous driver.

"Pull over there," Hanna directed his man. We stopped at a sign that said "Mary's coffee shop," fifty feet from the road. The waitress inside was young and pretty. "What can I get you?" she asked us, her eyelashes fluttering. I figured tips must have been bad that day.

"Coffee," Hanna said, "and a jelly donut."

My father and Gary said "The same."

I said, "A hamburger and a large coke with ice."

We spent a half hour in the restaurant. Hanna was doing most of the talking but got up after a few minutes to make a phone call. He returned to our table, smiling and talking about the prospects for buying some cars at the auctions.

Meanwhile, my mind drifted toward thinking about Judy, the girl back in Miami I had taken out a few months before. She had stopped me recently outside my English class at Miami High to ask me why I hadn't called her since our first and only date.

"I'd like to read more of your South Sea story," she had said. I started to feel guilty about not calling her but I spent the remainder of the time at the coffee shop trying to forget her, and looking up the dress of the cute blond waitress as she reached over the pickup counter to retrieve her orders. We left before I could see much beyond the black garters that kept her stockings up.

In a light drizzle, we climbed back into the car. Gary assured us we would now make Jacksonville, our next major stop, by two thirty or three in the afternoon. Over coffee, I had noted that he had lightened up a lot and was telling us stories about his experiences in the army. I started to feel more relaxed around him as we sped past scrub grass, numerous small palms, a few snakes and lizards, an egret or two, and even a large chicken that seemed to be sunning itself at the side of the road. This was Florida at its finest. I had finally gotten out of Buffalo for good and landed in Paradise.

Every so often, the ocean flew by on my right, blue and green in color, coming into view between the mounds of sand. Then it would suddenly disappear like in a magician's trick as our car fell below sea level. But I knew the ocean was still there. It would be so for a thousand years, always on the right when you traveled North. My friend, Ray Heller in Miami had taught me that. "You can never get lost in Florida," he had said, "if you know where the ocean is."

I wondered why Ray knew so many things at his age and why he was not afraid of anything. I wanted to be like that but something was standing in my way. Someday I would be like that, I told myself. There were many things I wanted to change about myself and time was on my side. I was only seventeen.

I was now at the window seat, watching the small fishing towns of Stuart and Melbourne fly by, and then bigger towns like Daytona Beach which took longer. My watch said it was two o'clock.

"We'll be in Jacksonville before you know it," Hanna said to me, then nodded in a strange sort of way to my father who put his hand on my shoulder.

"Lee," my father said. "I was thinking of giving you a special present for your birthday coming up." he said. "Actually, Mr. Hanna has a lot to do with it."

Hanna looked at me and cleared his throat. "You know, your

father and I wanted you to come along on this trip for a reason. I never had a son. Or any children for that matter."

I wondered what he was driving at. Maybe he wanted to adopt me.

"I remember how it was when I was seventeen," Hanna continued. "I didn't even have a girl friend then. But I know you like girls from the way I saw you looking at the waitress at that coffee shop, back there."

I blushed. He was starting to get a little too personal, and I didn't know why.

"Have you ever been with a girl?"

"Sure," I said too quickly, embarrassed at the question. I might be a virgin but I had kissed plenty of girls including Sally probably a hundred times or more.

"I mean all the way," Hanna said.

"Well, not really, if that's what you mean," I said, correcting myself. My father knew the truth and I wasn't about to start lying about it.

Sounding as uncomfortable as I felt, my father cut into the conversation. "Look, Lee, Mr. Hanna knows a woman in Jacksonville he's very friendly with. She stays at the Hotel Mayflower. We're going to stop there for something to eat and you could go up and see her while we're eating. Would you like to do that? Do you know what I mean?"

I felt a little twinge of excitement…and annoyance. Naturally I knew what he meant. I'm a virgin, not a moron, I reminded myself silently. "Yes, Dad, I do," I said sarcastically.

Hanna said, "I think you do too," he smiled, squeezing my shoulder. "So… it's all settled. I took the liberty of calling her ahead just in case you wanted to go up and see her. All right?"

"Okay," I said.

And then we were in St. John's county with the St. John's river to our left, and Jacksonville in the distance under a damp sky, and I thought of the mysterious phone call Hanna had made from the restaurant, knowing now who he had been talking to, the girl who would change my life. Was she old ? Was she my age? Was she pretty? Did I really care?

At the Mayflower we went directly to the main restaurant, a decent place with cloth napkins and silver wear on the table. Hanna, my father and Gary sat down. I was about to also when Hanna waved me off and gave me a key from his pocket.

"This is a key to Room 302. Claire will be up in a few minutes. She'll take care of you."

He shook my hand. My father squeezed my shoulder and said "Good luck, son," then slipped ten dollars into my hand while I smiled nervously at the man I apparently didn't know very well and couldn't remember ever calling me "son."

On the elevator to the third floor, I wondered exactly what Dennis Morgan would have done in this situation? Strangely, as I left the elevator and then turned the key in the lock of the hotel room door, a song Morgan had once sung in the movie "The Great Ziegfeld" kept running through my mind:

"A pretty girl ...is like a melody
that haunts you ...night and day"

In the room, I nervously unbuttoned and removed my shirt in front of the mirror, revealing a hairless chest and muscles on my arms not nearly as big as I wanted. They would have to do if I was to impress Claire. But why did I have to impress her anyway ? She was a prostitute. I'd never see her again. I put my shirt on and removed the ten dollar bill from my pocket, throwing the money onto the bed. Was that too obvious? Maybe Claire would take some kind of offense. And then, again, maybe the soft knock I heard on the door wasn't her at all, but the house detective with a gun wondering what the devil I was doing in a room all by myself , and waiting… for what? I grabbed the money, put it back in my pocket and slowly opened the door.

Standing in front of me was a well dressed woman, about forty. In her hand was a lit cigarette. It was better than a smoking gun, I thought.

"Hello," she said with a pleasant Southern accent, maybe Georgia or Alabama. She glided over to a chair across the room like she was on roller skates. "I'm Claire. Ralph said you wanted to see me about something," she said.

Something? Was I supposed to tell her what she was there for? But I kept quiet since she was pretty in a classy sort of way, with short, dark hair curled around her face and I liked the way she smiled.

She removed each shoe with the other foot and sat down, crossing her tanned, bare legs. It was annoying that she seemed so completely relaxed while I felt cold sweat gathering under my arms and down my back.

She took a long drag on her cigarette, then put it out.

"And you're Lee, " she said.

"Yes," I said. "Is Claire your real name?"

"No one ever asked me that. But that's okay. Actually, It's Hildi, but I like Claire much better."

"You look a little like Lana Turner in a movie I saw once," I said.

"We girls all look alike with our clothes off, so why don't I start taking mine off. Feel free to take your pant's off at anytime before I leave. I suppose this is your first time?"

"Sort of," I said.

She nodded, unbuttoning her blouse, and removing her skirt.

I stood there motionless.

"You'll have to take your pants off, if we're going to get through this," she said. "Unless you know something I don't."

Embarrassed, I unhooked my belt and zipper allowing my pants to drop to my ankles. Standing there, I was sure I looked something like Charlie Chaplin unraveling in one of his silent films. I stepped out of my pants.

"You forgot a few things," she said.

"You still have your things on," I countered, finding my voice. Two could play at this game.

"Not for long," she said.

She got up and took off her bra and panties. I thought the smell of roses had drifted across the room.

"Haven't you ever seen a naked woman?"

"Sure," I said.

"Your mother? ... Okay, forget I said that. It's been a long day."

She walked over and led me into the bathroom for a quick wash, then over to the bed. We laid down and the rest was history. Not stupendous, monumental history like the Civil War or the attack on Pearl harbor or Superman's flight to Germany to capture Hitler which I read about when I was young. But just good enough to make me walk two steps at a time down the stairs (not taking the elevator) at the Mayflower Hotel in 1951 and face the smiling reviewing committee.

"Well?" my father said. "How was it?"

"It was great," I lied.

"Nice girl, huh? " Hanna said.

"Yes," I said. "Nice girl."

125

Chapter twenty two

An expensive itch

No longer burdened by sexual inexperience, I slept easily for the last leg of our trip, opening my eyes just as we entered the sleepy Georgia town that seemed to be reluctant to enter the twentieth century. Farmers in overalls walked along the street with cow manure on their shoes. Horses roamed in meadows, refreshing themselves on strands of grass in the fields, while chickens clucked happily in backyards, laying large white Georgia eggs.

At five in the afternoon, after checking into what appeared to be the only hotel in town, the four of us drove to the giant car barns down the road where the auctions were held.

It was hot inside and we started wiping the sweat off our heads and necks. After receiving a qualifying number, we stood near the auctioneer, a wily looking man who spoke so fast and unintelligibly, I thought he was speaking Mandarin Chinese.

"Now three hundred, three hundred, three fifty, four hundred, now chung fu yung," he said rapidly. I thought I saw sparks fly from his mouth. He might be having a stroke.

In the back, studying the outlines of a late model Chevrolet with a slight dent in the right fender, my father and I stood quietly assessing the situation. Closer to the action, Hanna and Gary evaluated other cars rolling up to the spotlight. While I was trying to decode the lightning fast words coming from the stage, the auctioneer had apparently fixed his eyes on the "new man" in town, my father. He looked over our way several times, while several late model cars, all nicely polished, were driven up for inspection. Occasionally a hand would rise from the crowd, the hammer would drop and the auctioneer hollered "sold," to somebody.

Around this time, I noticed my father was sweating profusely. He was looking nervously this way and that way, playing the part of the experienced car dealer, carefully studying the merchandise. I could see he was itching to buy something before he passed out from the heat. Yet when a good looking black, 1948 Cadillac sedan, above his price range, was brought up for inspection, my father was barely aware of the new arrival. His attention was centered on another matter: a Georgia fly searching for water had perched itself on the perspiration saturated bald spot of my father's head. The large insect was drinking his fill when my father's hand suddenly shot up to eliminate the unbearable irritation. At that exact moment, the auctioneer, spying a single hand moving vertically toward the roof, banged his gavel on the table with the following announcement made over the loud speaker : "Sold to Honest Abe's for twenty five hundred dollars."

By the time my father looked around in confusion to see if there was another dealer using his name, it was too late. Too embarrassed to protest and hoping he had not paid too much, he had bought a car without meaning too. It had turned out to be a very expensive itch.

Chapter twenty three

Out of the blue and into the night

In 1952, I should have been, and was, for a while, happier than a Miami Beach clam at low tide. In June, I was graduating from Miami Senior High School and would be looking back on the more than two years I had spent in Miami as the best years of my life. My expectations were high as I planned to ask my father about starting at the University of Miami in the fall.

As a matter of fact, in February, I and several of my AZA brothers had been "rushed" hard by a Jewish fraternity at the University and had showed up for a wild party at the Sorrento Hotel on the Beach. Indulging ourselves on fried chicken and a barrel of beer, we had gotten drunk and then watched a couple of raw movies, one entitled "Over the hump to get some rump," and the other, "The dentist drills," none of them destined to be Academy Award nominees.

Also that month, I had taken part in the annual Miami High Jamboree which featured selected parts of Jerome Kern's Showboat and numerous individual acts, one of which was my singing of Johnnie Ray's famous ballad "I won't cry anymore." If I had only known that night what my parents in a few months were about to tell me I might have surprised everyone in the audience with some real tears.

The bad news arrived in May. My father announced that he had lost most of his money in the used car business and we were returning to Buffalo. There was no need for further discussion. Reality had intervened in my carefully thought out plans to live in paradise. Why was I so surprised? Had I not ignored the late night whispers about the business losing money? About the weak economy? If I had listened I might have heard the talk about Sullivan, our sales manager, who had overpaid other dealers for cars, and my father's suspicion that he might have received kickbacks under the table. Maybe my mother had been right about people who drank too much.

There were some positives. In the first family conference I could ever remember, my father talked quietly about our future: He was still able to practice law in Buffalo and draw on his ability as a trial lawyer. Also, he had certain contacts in Buffalo who would help him once we returned. It would not be that hard to find a partner, probably an older lawyer with an established practice who needed help in trying cases. This could be the start of a comeback. As for me, I would start at the University of Buffalo while my mother presumably would return to her club work. Everything seemed to be settled, neatly tied up in a box with a pretty bow around it. All except the fact that I was miserable.

Still, in June, I graduated and my mother began preparing for the return to Buffalo, while my father cleaned up his business affairs, sold off his inventory, and paid off whatever he still owed the bank. The lease on the Eighth Street lot was up in July so that represented no problem, nor did the lease on our duplex apartment on S.W. 29TH Street, which would mature in early August, a week before we were going to depart.

For weeks as 'D" day approached, I had trouble coping with what now appeared to be inevitable. Ray Heller, who I thought had the answer to everything, had no solution. What did I really expect? He was, after all, only eighteen and uncertain about his own future.

Every day, I drove around alone in the "green Hornet," trying to think of my alternatives. Staying behind, I'd need enough money to survive without my parent's support. Was it possible I could convert the part time bag boy job I had at Food Fair into a full time position? Or sell shoes at A.S. Beck on Lincoln Road in Miami Beach where my mother had occasionally shopped? Was there any chance that I could make enough part time to go to college and get an education on my own? My father's words kept presenting themselves in my brain: "A man without an education is like a rowboat with oars." Unfortunately, I didn't even have enough money to buy the rowboat.

I drove aimlessly around through the wonderful summer smells of Jasmine and salt air, past the columns of Miami High School and memories of "Stingaree" days, down Coral Way to the lush Venetian Pool where my AZA brothers and I had swam after school and looked for dates.

On Biscayne Blvd, one day, I headed toward the studio of my singing teacher, Ms. Morris, wanting to talk. I parked my car on the street and walked in. She was there, as always, sitting alone at the piano, as beautiful and as wise as ever.

"I suppose part of life is what happens when one isn't paying much attention," she said philosophically, when I told her I probably would have to return to Buffalo. "But I know you love Florida as much as I do," she said, "and therefore you'll be back.

You know, once you get sand in your shoes, you can never get it out. Now go back to Buffalo, make the best of it, get an education and keep on singing. It's good for the soul."

She had told me what I wanted to hear. I kissed her on the cheek, small payment for invaluable advice. I would go back to the city of my birth, and "damn the torpedoes," as one of my favorite movies stars had once said, a long time ago. I'd be the man my father had always wanted me to be. But very quietly, I thought, I would also wait for the day when I'd get out of Buffalo for real, and return to my very special "island." Another family secret.